PELÉ

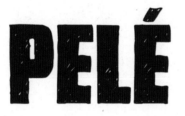

PELÉ
THE KING OF SOCCER

Written by
EDDY SIMON

Illustrated by
VINCENT BRASCAGLIA

:01
First Second
NEW YORK

Chapter 1
A Day in 1950

"If I close my eyes, I can still see my first soccer ball."
—Pelé, September 2013

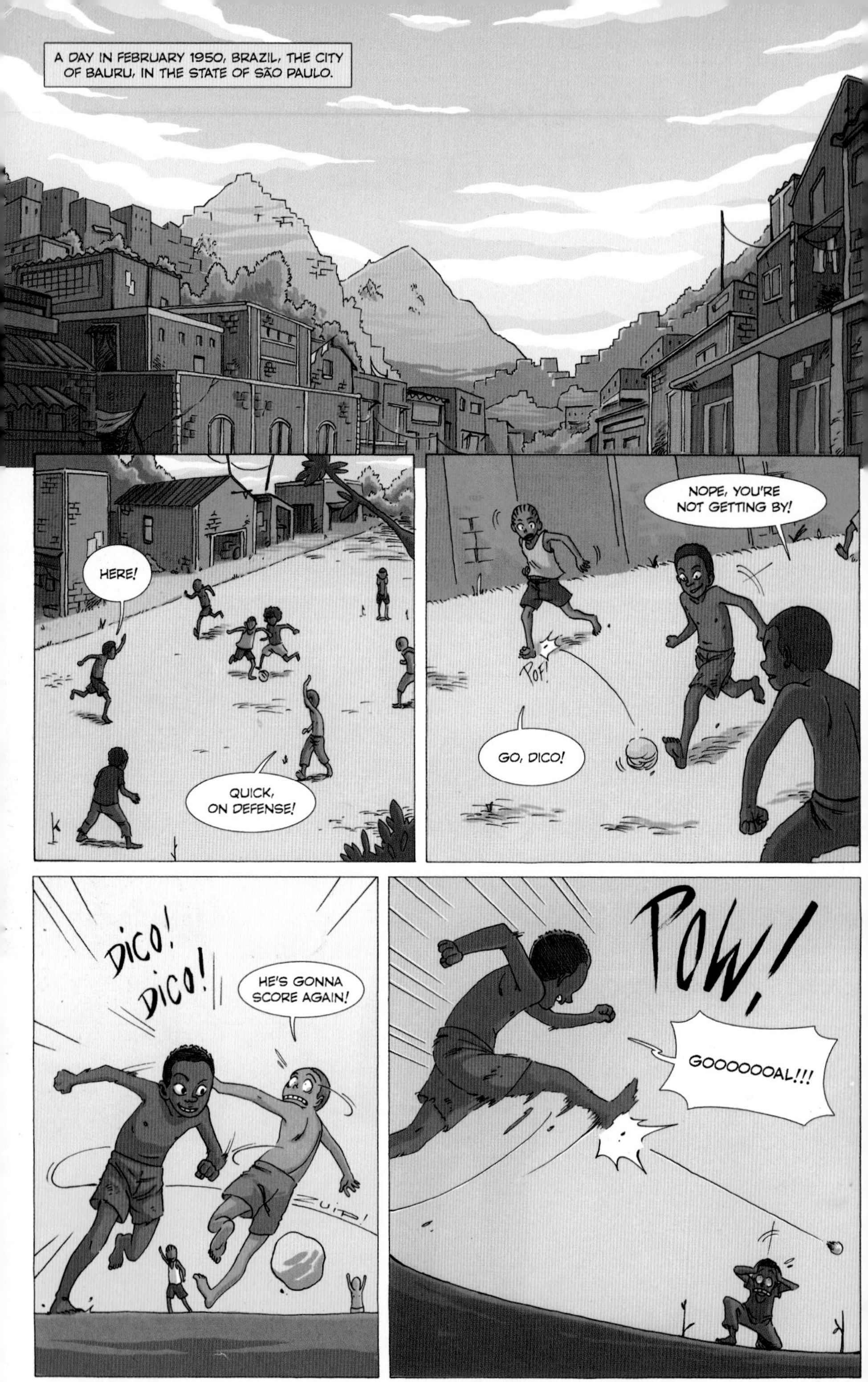

A DAY IN FEBRUARY 1950, BRAZIL, THE CITY OF BAURU, IN THE STATE OF SÃO PAULO.
HERE!
QUICK, ON DEFENSE!
NOPE, YOU'RE NOT GETTING BY!
POF!
GO, DICO!
DICO! DICO!
HE'S GONNA SCORE AGAIN!
POW!
GOOOOOOAL!!!

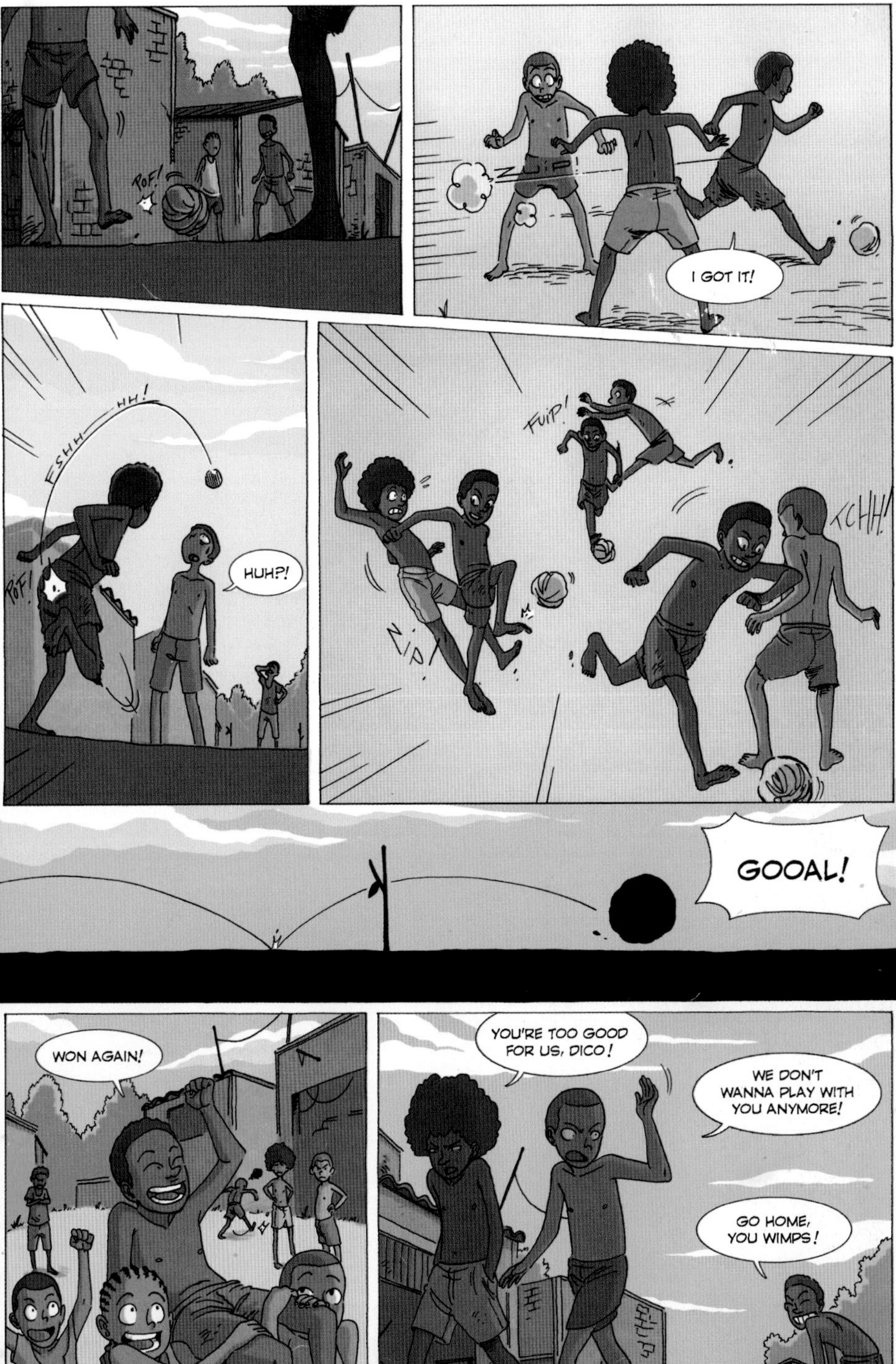
POF!
ZUP!
I GOT IT!
FSHHHH!
POF!
HUH?!
FUIP!
TCHH!
ZIP!
GOOAL!
WON AGAIN!
BEM FEITO,*
GASOLINA!
YOU'RE TOO GOOD
FOR US, DICO!
WE DON'T
WANNA PLAY WITH
YOU ANYMORE!
GO HOME,
YOU WIMPS!

*GOOD JOB.

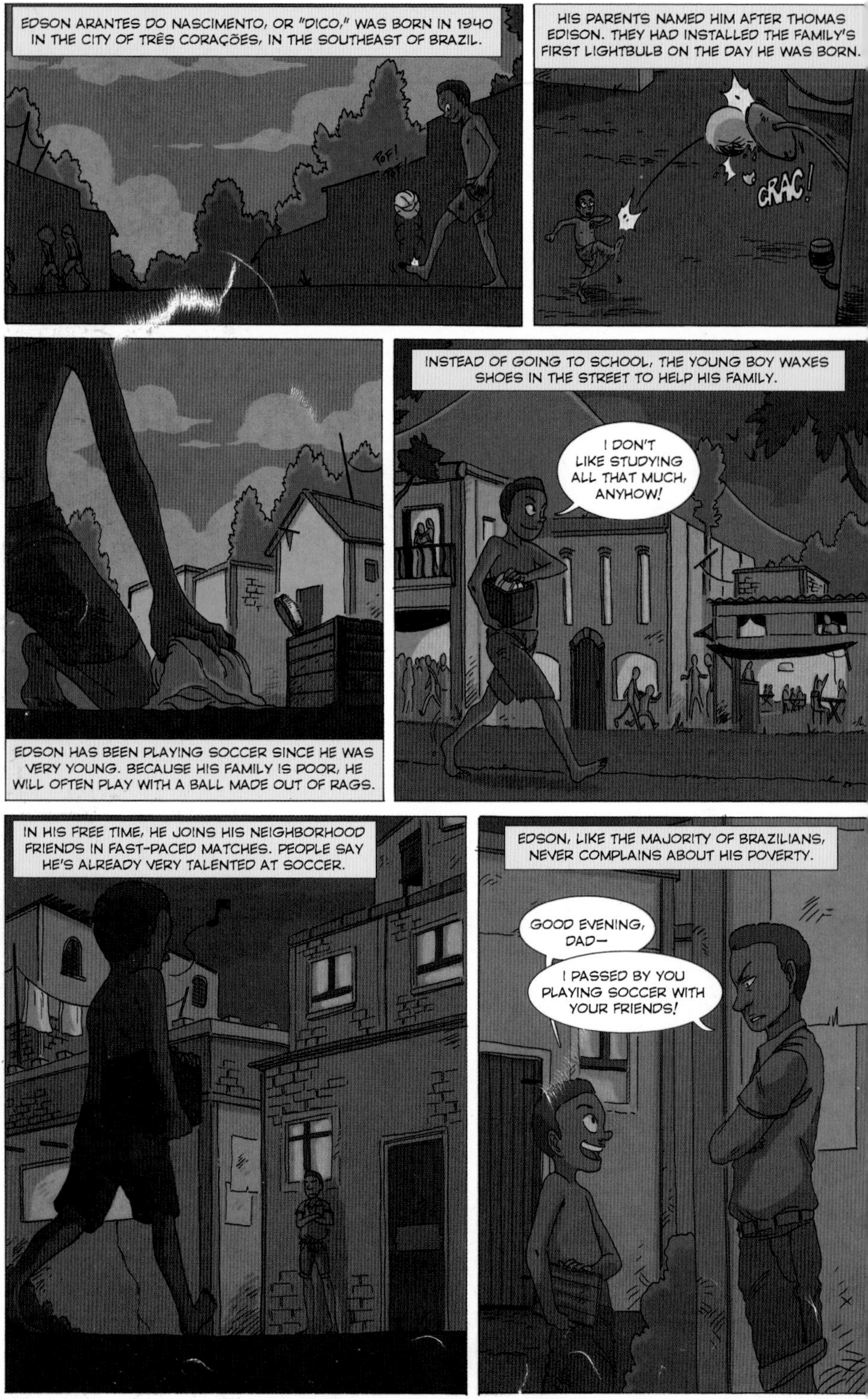
EDSON ARANTES DO NASCIMENTO, OR "DICO," WAS BORN IN 1940 IN THE CITY OF TRÊS CORAÇÕES, IN THE SOUTHEAST OF BRAZIL.
HIS PARENTS NAMED HIM AFTER THOMAS EDISON. THEY HAD INSTALLED THE FAMILY'S FIRST LIGHTBULB ON THE DAY HE WAS BORN.
CRAC!
EDSON HAS BEEN PLAYING SOCCER SINCE HE WAS VERY YOUNG. BECAUSE HIS FAMILY IS POOR, HE WILL OFTEN PLAY WITH A BALL MADE OUT OF RAGS.
INSTEAD OF GOING TO SCHOOL, THE YOUNG BOY WAXES SHOES IN THE STREET TO HELP HIS FAMILY.
I DON'T LIKE STUDYING ALL THAT MUCH, ANYHOW!
IN HIS FREE TIME, HE JOINS HIS NEIGHBORHOOD FRIENDS IN FAST-PACED MATCHES. PEOPLE SAY HE'S ALREADY VERY TALENTED AT SOCCER.
EDSON, LIKE THE MAJORITY OF BRAZILIANS, NEVER COMPLAINS ABOUT HIS POVERTY.
GOOD EVENING, DAD—
I PASSED BY YOU PLAYING SOCCER WITH YOUR FRIENDS!

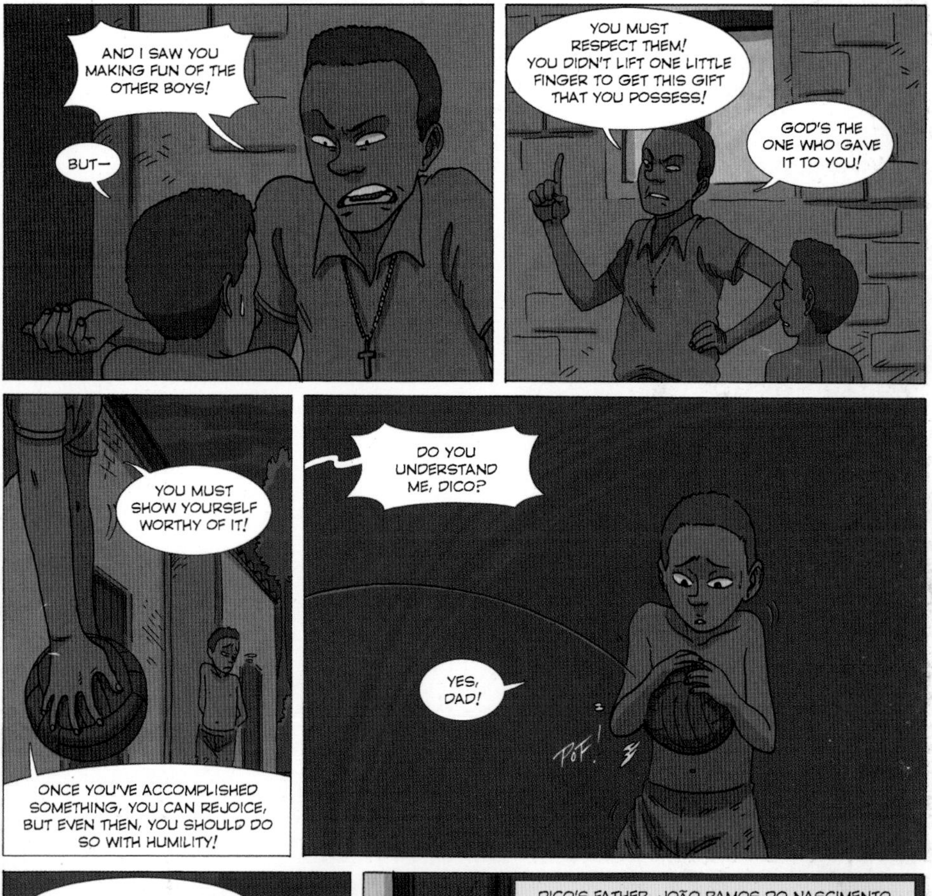

AND I SAW YOU MAKING FUN OF THE OTHER BOYS!
BUT—
YOU MUST RESPECT THEM! YOU DIDN'T LIFT ONE LITTLE FINGER TO GET THIS GIFT THAT YOU POSSESS!
GOD'S THE ONE WHO GAVE IT TO YOU!
YOU MUST SHOW YOURSELF WORTHY OF IT!
ONCE YOU'VE ACCOMPLISHED SOMETHING, YOU CAN REJOICE, BUT EVEN THEN, YOU SHOULD DO SO WITH HUMILITY!
DO YOU UNDERSTAND ME, DICO?
YES, DAD!
POF!
OH! WHAT'S THIS?! A REAL LEATHER BALL!
HEH-HEH! SURPRISE!
DICO'S FATHER, JOÃO RAMOS DO NASCIMENTO, OR "DONDINHO," IS ORIGINALLY FROM THE STATE OF MINAS GERAIS, A REGION WHERE PEOPLE LABOR TO EXTRACT METALS* FROM AN ARID LAND.
ALL RIGHT. COME AND PRACTICE BEHIND THE HOUSE!

*GOLD, IN PARTICULAR, DURING THE COLONIAL ERA.

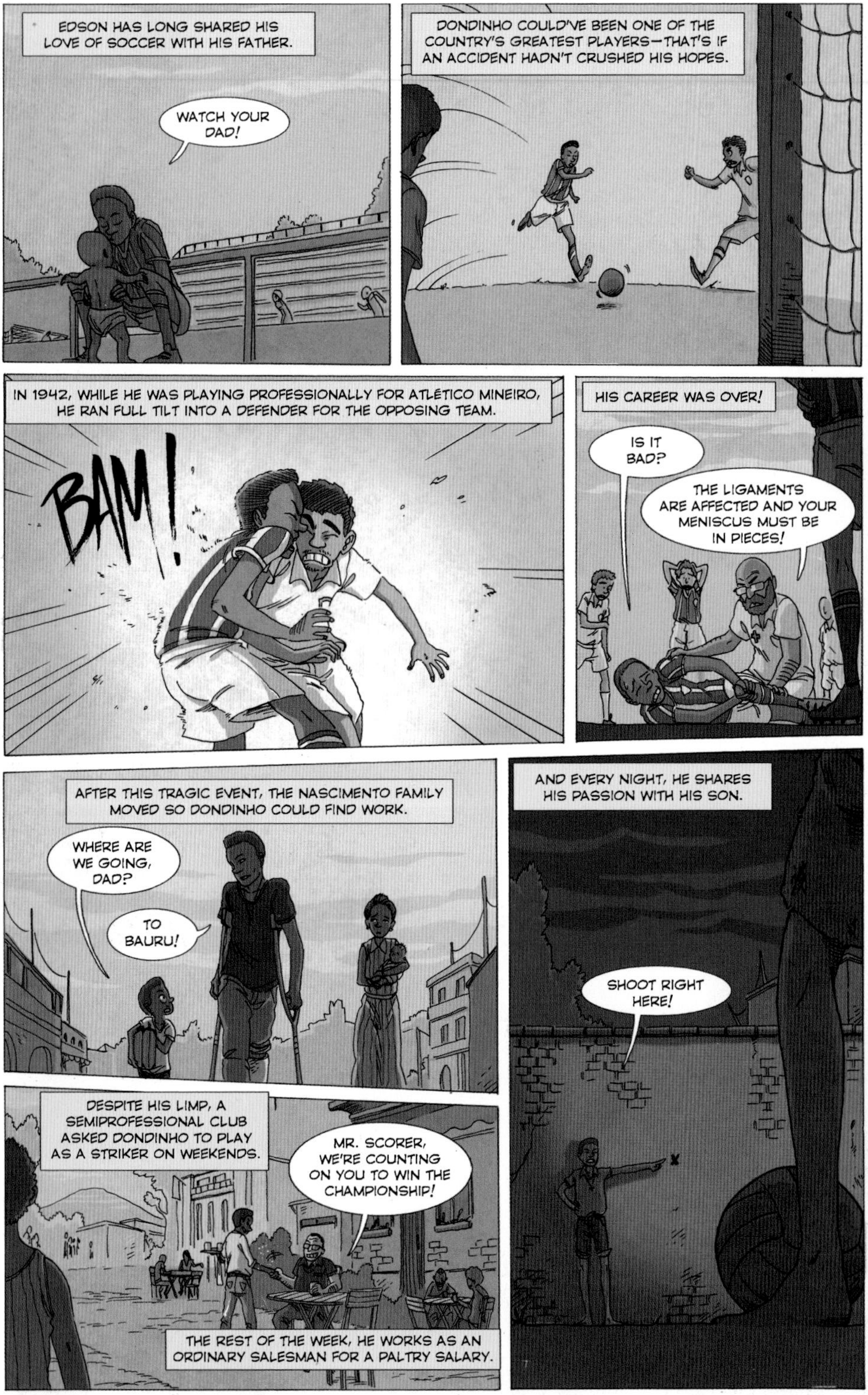
EDSON HAS LONG SHARED HIS LOVE OF SOCCER WITH HIS FATHER.
WATCH YOUR DAD!
DONDINHO COULD'VE BEEN ONE OF THE COUNTRY'S GREATEST PLAYERS—THAT'S IF AN ACCIDENT HADN'T CRUSHED HIS HOPES.
IN 1942, WHILE HE WAS PLAYING PROFESSIONALLY FOR ATLÉTICO MINEIRO, HE RAN FULL TILT INTO A DEFENDER FOR THE OPPOSING TEAM.
BAM!
HIS CAREER WAS OVER!
IS IT BAD?
THE LIGAMENTS ARE AFFECTED AND YOUR MENISCUS MUST BE IN PIECES!
AFTER THIS TRAGIC EVENT, THE NASCIMENTO FAMILY MOVED SO DONDINHO COULD FIND WORK.
WHERE ARE WE GOING, DAD?
TO BAURU!
DESPITE HIS LIMP, A SEMIPROFESSIONAL CLUB ASKED DONDINHO TO PLAY AS A STRIKER ON WEEKENDS.
MR. SCORER, WE'RE COUNTING ON YOU TO WIN THE CHAMPIONSHIP!
THE REST OF THE WEEK, HE WORKS AS AN ORDINARY SALESMAN FOR A PALTRY SALARY.
AND EVERY NIGHT, HE SHARES HIS PASSION WITH HIS SON.
SHOOT RIGHT HERE!

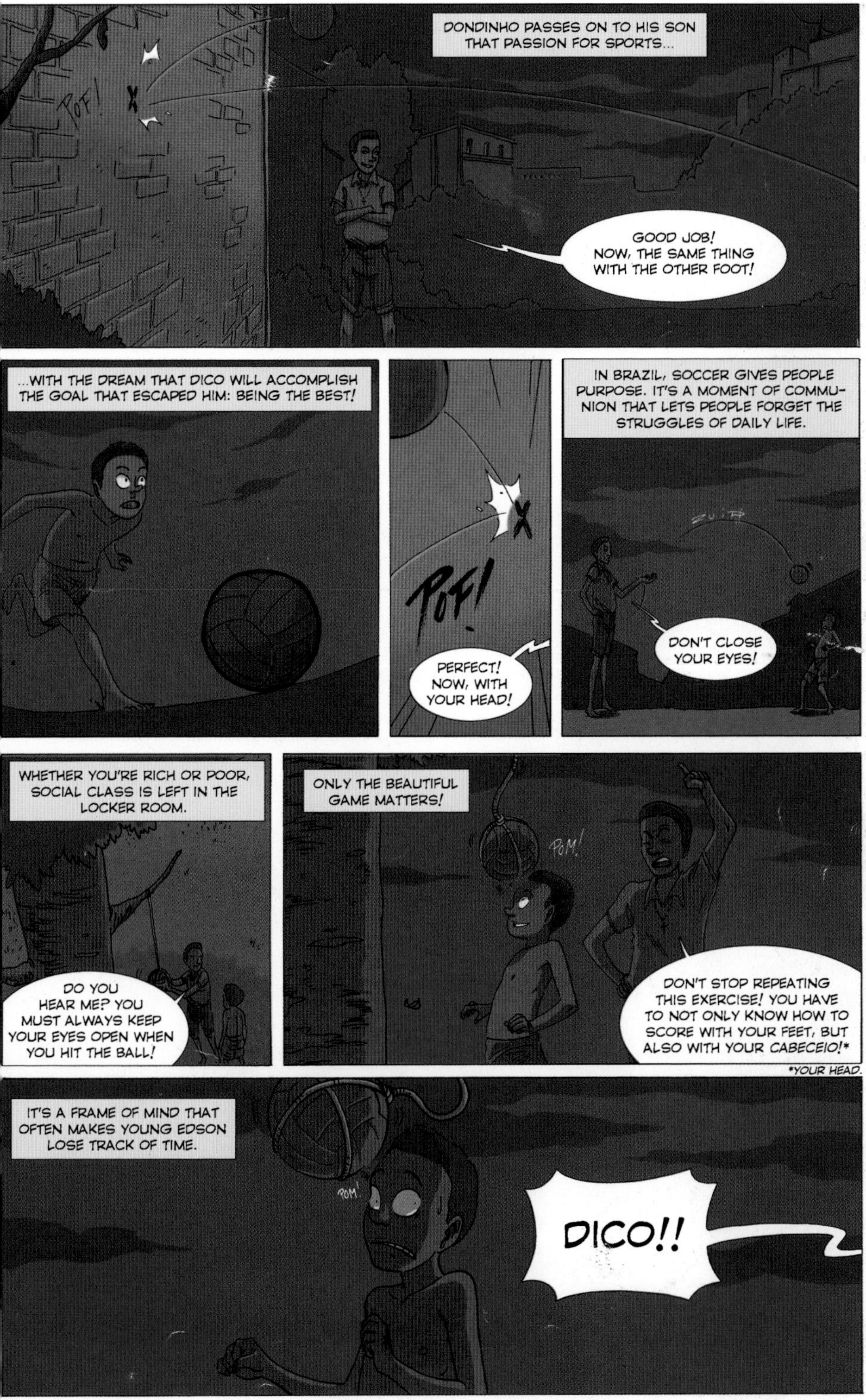
DONDINHO PASSES ON TO HIS SON THAT PASSION FOR SPORTS...
POF!
GOOD JOB! NOW, THE SAME THING WITH THE OTHER FOOT!
...WITH THE DREAM THAT DICO WILL ACCOMPLISH THE GOAL THAT ESCAPED HIM: BEING THE BEST!
POF!
PERFECT! NOW, WITH YOUR HEAD!
IN BRAZIL, SOCCER GIVES PEOPLE PURPOSE. IT'S A MOMENT OF COMMU-NION THAT LETS PEOPLE FORGET THE STRUGGLES OF DAILY LIFE.
DON'T CLOSE YOUR EYES!
WHETHER YOU'RE RICH OR POOR, SOCIAL CLASS IS LEFT IN THE LOCKER ROOM.
DO YOU HEAR ME? YOU MUST ALWAYS KEEP YOUR EYES OPEN WHEN YOU HIT THE BALL!
ONLY THE BEAUTIFUL GAME MATTERS!
POM!
DON'T STOP REPEATING THIS EXERCISE! YOU HAVE TO NOT ONLY KNOW HOW TO SCORE WITH YOUR FEET, BUT ALSO WITH YOUR CABECEIO!*
*YOUR HEAD.
IT'S A FRAME OF MIND THAT OFTEN MAKES YOUNG EDSON LOSE TRACK OF TIME.
POM!
DICO!!

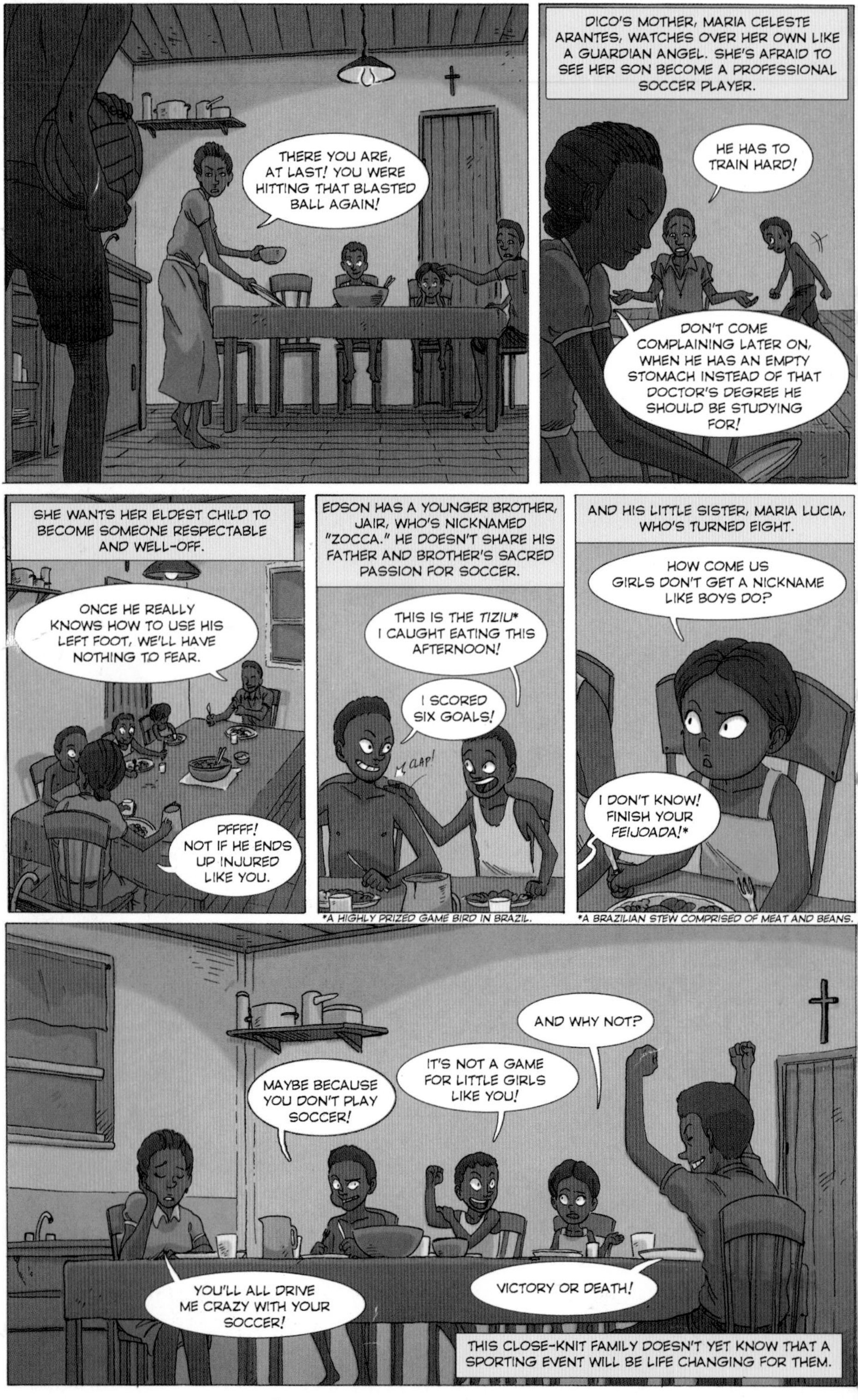
THERE YOU ARE, AT LAST! YOU WERE HITTING THAT BLASTED BALL AGAIN!
DICO'S MOTHER, MARIA CELESTE ARANTES, WATCHES OVER HER OWN LIKE A GUARDIAN ANGEL. SHE'S AFRAID TO SEE HER SON BECOME A PROFESSIONAL SOCCER PLAYER.
HE HAS TO TRAIN HARD!
DON'T COME COMPLAINING LATER ON, WHEN HE HAS AN EMPTY STOMACH INSTEAD OF THAT DOCTOR'S DEGREE HE SHOULD BE STUDYING FOR!
SHE WANTS HER ELDEST CHILD TO BECOME SOMEONE RESPECTABLE AND WELL-OFF.
ONCE HE REALLY KNOWS HOW TO USE HIS LEFT FOOT, WE'LL HAVE NOTHING TO FEAR.
PFFFF! NOT IF HE ENDS UP INJURED LIKE YOU.
EDSON HAS A YOUNGER BROTHER, JAIR, WHO'S NICKNAMED "ZOCCA." HE DOESN'T SHARE HIS FATHER AND BROTHER'S SACRED PASSION FOR SOCCER.
THIS IS THE *TIZIU** I CAUGHT EATING THIS AFTERNOON!
I SCORED SIX GOALS!
CLAP!
*A HIGHLY PRIZED GAME BIRD IN BRAZIL.
AND HIS LITTLE SISTER, MARIA LUCIA, WHO'S TURNED EIGHT.
HOW COME US GIRLS DON'T GET A NICKNAME LIKE BOYS DO?
I DON'T KNOW! FINISH YOUR *FEIJOADA!**
*A BRAZILIAN STEW COMPRISED OF MEAT AND BEANS.
MAYBE BECAUSE YOU DON'T PLAY SOCCER!
IT'S NOT A GAME FOR LITTLE GIRLS LIKE YOU!
AND WHY NOT?
YOU'LL ALL DRIVE ME CRAZY WITH YOUR SOCCER!
VICTORY OR DEATH!
THIS CLOSE-KNIT FAMILY DOESN'T YET KNOW THAT A SPORTING EVENT WILL BE LIFE CHANGING FOR THEM.

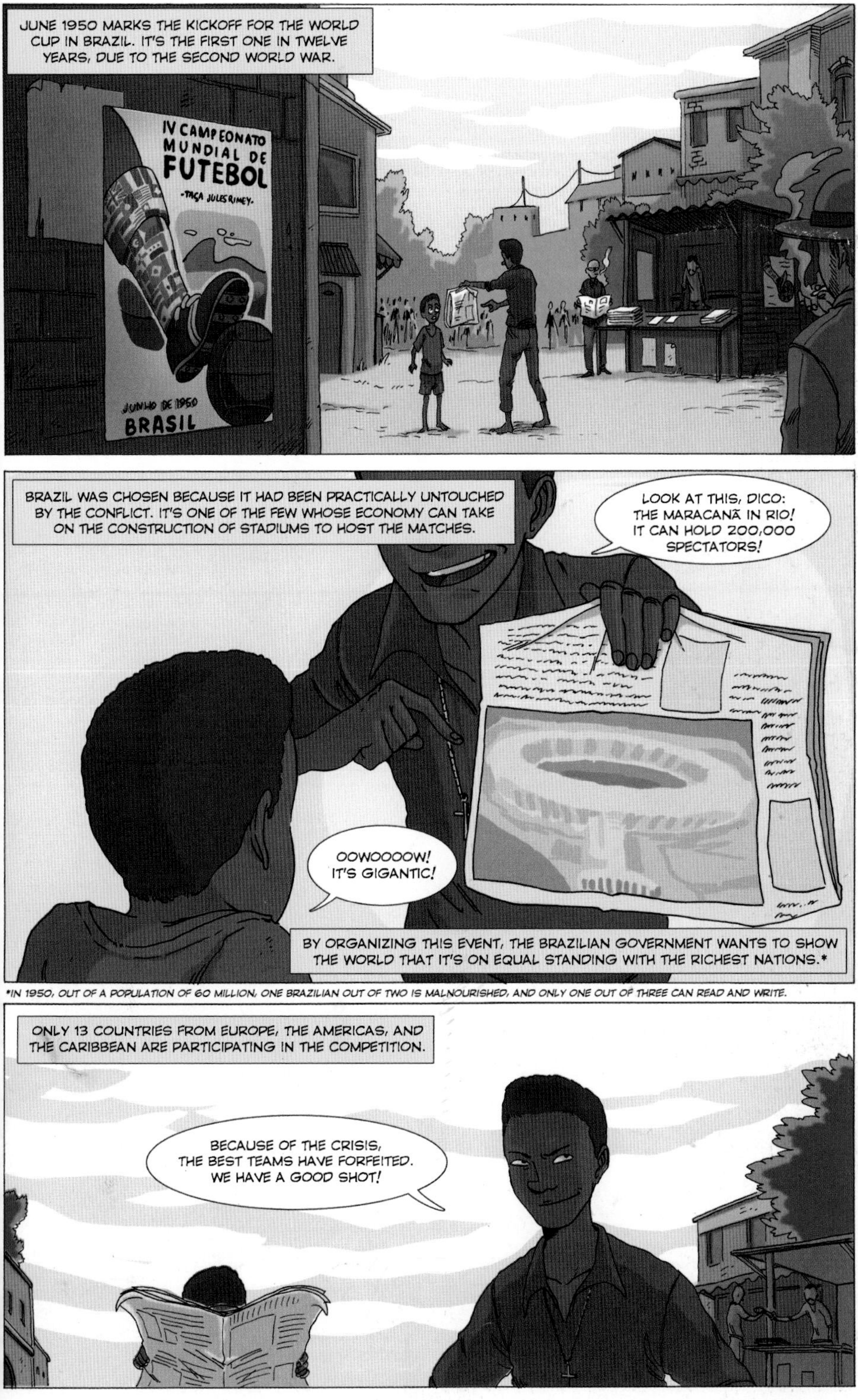

JUNE 1950 MARKS THE KICKOFF FOR THE WORLD CUP IN BRAZIL. IT'S THE FIRST ONE IN TWELVE YEARS, DUE TO THE SECOND WORLD WAR.
IV CAMPEONATO MUNDIAL DE FUTEBOL
-TAÇA JULES RIMEY-
JUNHO DE 1950
BRASIL
BRAZIL WAS CHOSEN BECAUSE IT HAD BEEN PRACTICALLY UNTOUCHED BY THE CONFLICT. IT'S ONE OF THE FEW WHOSE ECONOMY CAN TAKE ON THE CONSTRUCTION OF STADIUMS TO HOST THE MATCHES.
LOOK AT THIS, DICO: THE MARACANÃ IN RIO! IT CAN HOLD 200,000 SPECTATORS!
OOWOOOOW! IT'S GIGANTIC!
BY ORGANIZING THIS EVENT, THE BRAZILIAN GOVERNMENT WANTS TO SHOW THE WORLD THAT IT'S ON EQUAL STANDING WITH THE RICHEST NATIONS.*
*IN 1950, OUT OF A POPULATION OF 60 MILLION, ONE BRAZILIAN OUT OF TWO IS MALNOURISHED, AND ONLY ONE OUT OF THREE CAN READ AND WRITE.
ONLY 13 COUNTRIES FROM EUROPE, THE AMERICAS, AND THE CARIBBEAN ARE PARTICIPATING IN THE COMPETITION.
BECAUSE OF THE CRISIS, THE BEST TEAMS HAVE FORFEITED. WE HAVE A GOOD SHOT!

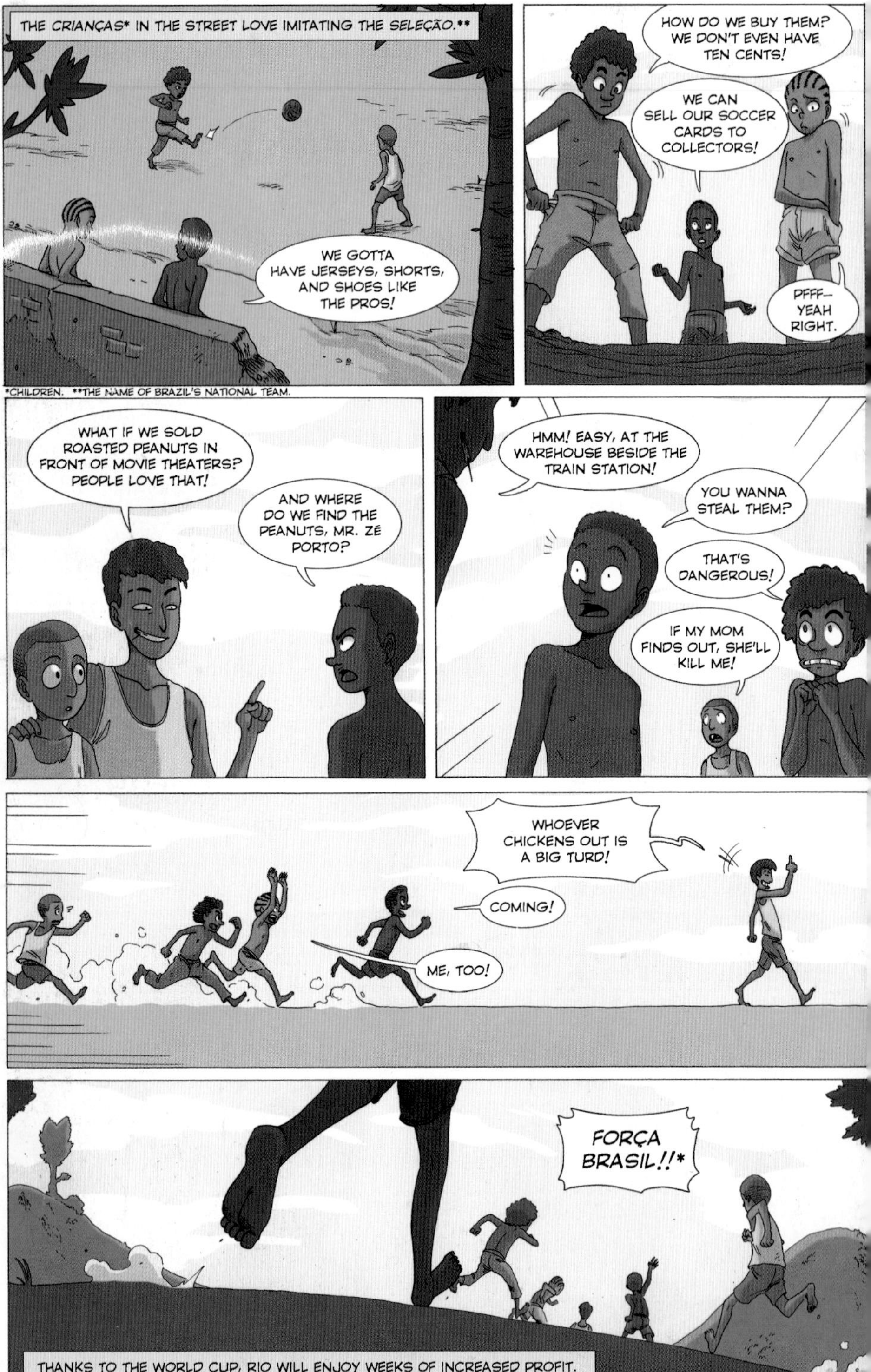
THE CRIANÇAS* IN THE STREET LOVE IMITATING THE SELEÇÃO.**
WE GOTTA HAVE JERSEYS, SHORTS, AND SHOES LIKE THE PROS!
HOW DO WE BUY THEM? WE DON'T EVEN HAVE TEN CENTS!
WE CAN SELL OUR SOCCER CARDS TO COLLECTORS!
PFFF— YEAH RIGHT.
*CHILDREN. **THE NAME OF BRAZIL'S NATIONAL TEAM.
WHAT IF WE SOLD ROASTED PEANUTS IN FRONT OF MOVIE THEATERS? PEOPLE LOVE THAT!
AND WHERE DO WE FIND THE PEANUTS, MR. ZÉ PORTO?
HMM! EASY, AT THE WAREHOUSE BESIDE THE TRAIN STATION!
YOU WANNA STEAL THEM?
THAT'S DANGEROUS!
IF MY MOM FINDS OUT, SHE'LL KILL ME!
WHOEVER CHICKENS OUT IS A BIG TURD!
COMING!
ME, TOO!
FORÇA BRASIL!!*
THANKS TO THE WORLD CUP, RIO WILL ENJOY WEEKS OF INCREASED PROFIT.
*BRAZIL STRONG

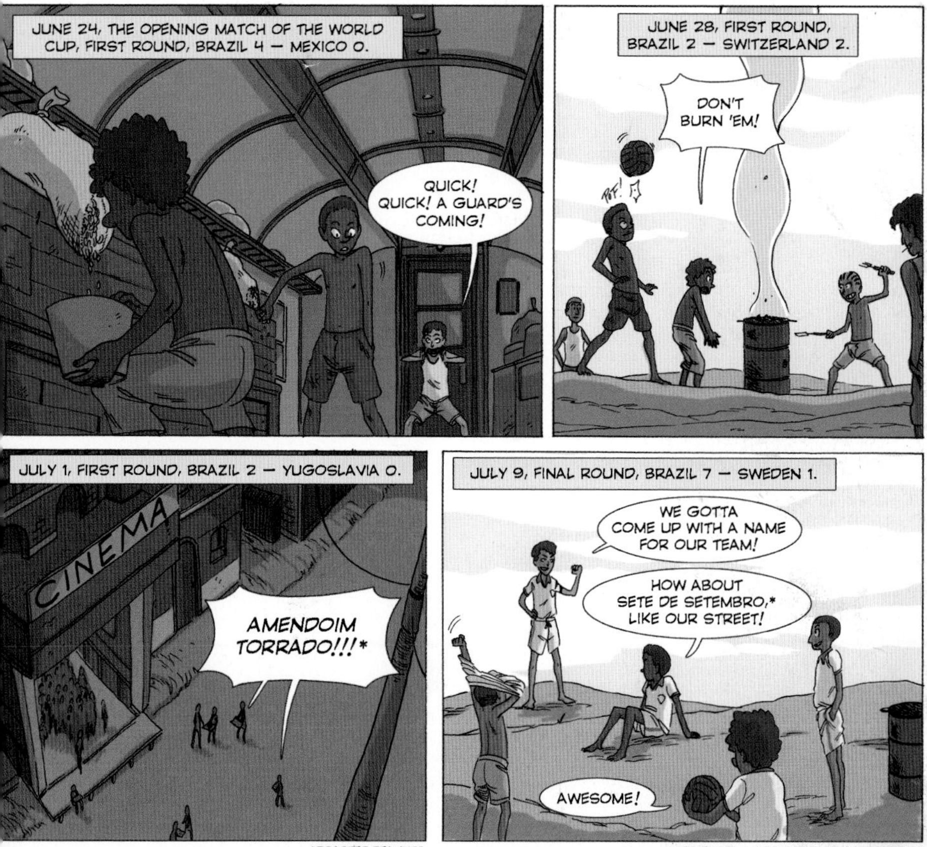

JUNE 24, THE OPENING MATCH OF THE WORLD CUP, FIRST ROUND, BRAZIL 4 — MEXICO 0.
QUICK! QUICK! A GUARD'S COMING!
JUNE 28, FIRST ROUND, BRAZIL 2 — SWITZERLAND 2.
DON'T BURN 'EM!
JULY 1, FIRST ROUND, BRAZIL 2 — YUGOSLAVIA 0.
CINEMA
AMENDOIM TORRADO!!!*
JULY 9, FINAL ROUND, BRAZIL 7 — SWEDEN 1.
WE GOTTA COME UP WITH A NAME FOR OUR TEAM!
HOW ABOUT SETE DE SETEMBRO,* LIKE OUR STREET!
AWESOME!

*ROASTED PEANUTS.

*SEPTEMBER 7, BRAZIL'S INDEPENDENCE DAY.

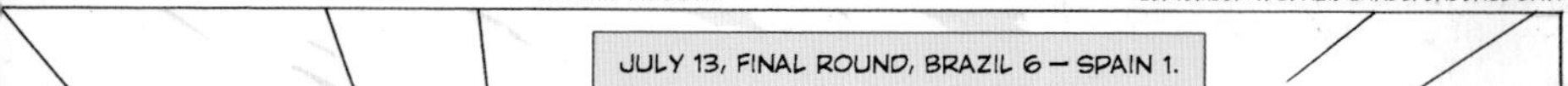

JULY 13, FINAL ROUND, BRAZIL 6 — SPAIN 1.
BRAZIL QUALIFIES!
POW!!

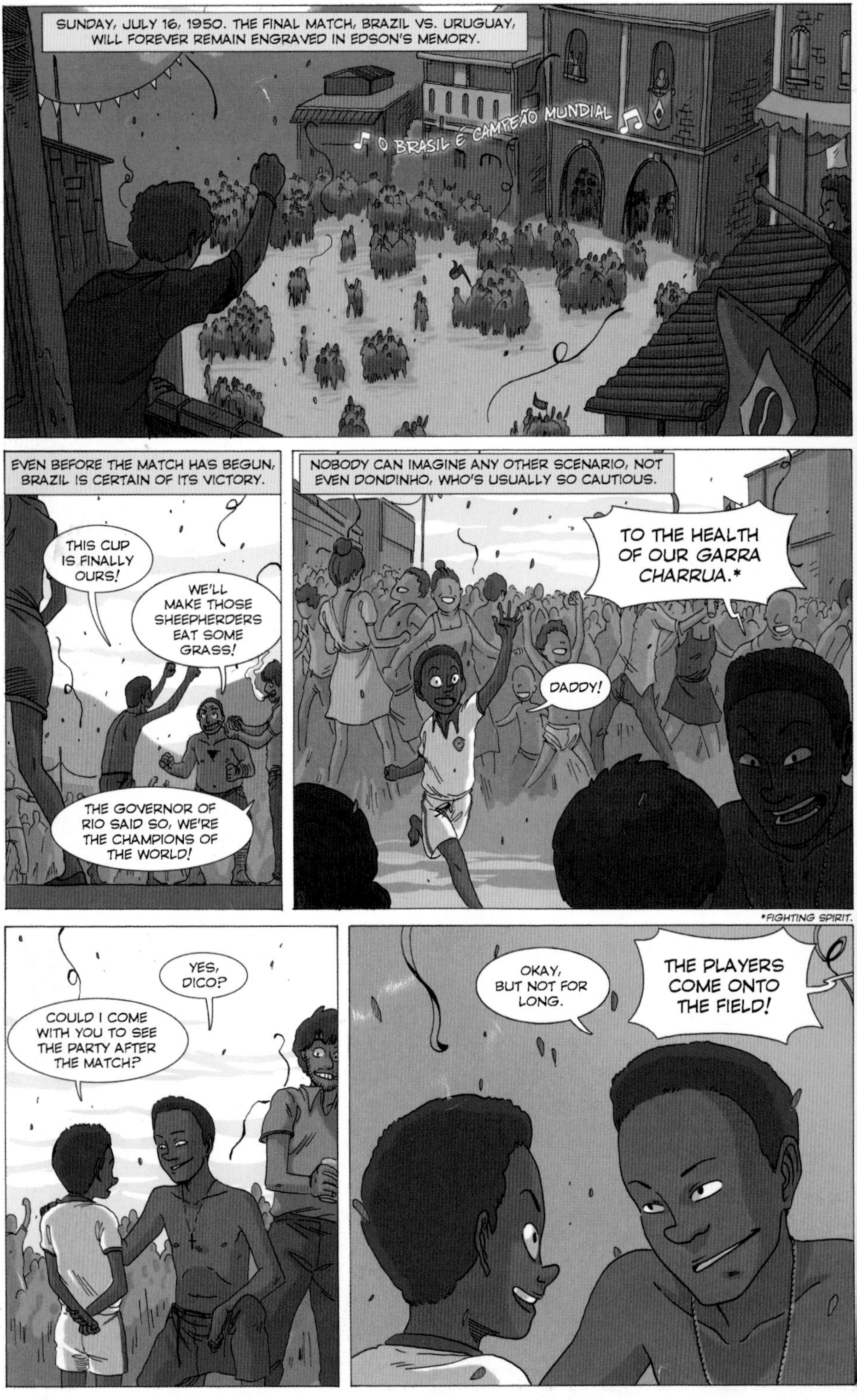
SUNDAY, JULY 16, 1950. THE FINAL MATCH, BRAZIL VS. URUGUAY, WILL FOREVER REMAIN ENGRAVED IN EDSON'S MEMORY.
♫ O BRASIL É CAMPEÃO MUNDIAL ♫
EVEN BEFORE THE MATCH HAS BEGUN, BRAZIL IS CERTAIN OF ITS VICTORY.
THIS CUP IS FINALLY OURS!
WE'LL MAKE THOSE SHEEPHERDERS EAT SOME GRASS!
THE GOVERNOR OF RIO SAID SO, WE'RE THE CHAMPIONS OF THE WORLD!
NOBODY CAN IMAGINE ANY OTHER SCENARIO, NOT EVEN DONDINHO, WHO'S USUALLY SO CAUTIOUS.
TO THE HEALTH OF OUR GARRA CHARRUA.*
DADDY!
*FIGHTING SPIRIT.
YES, DICO?
COULD I COME WITH YOU TO SEE THE PARTY AFTER THE MATCH?
OKAY, BUT NOT FOR LONG.
THE PLAYERS COME ONTO THE FIELD!

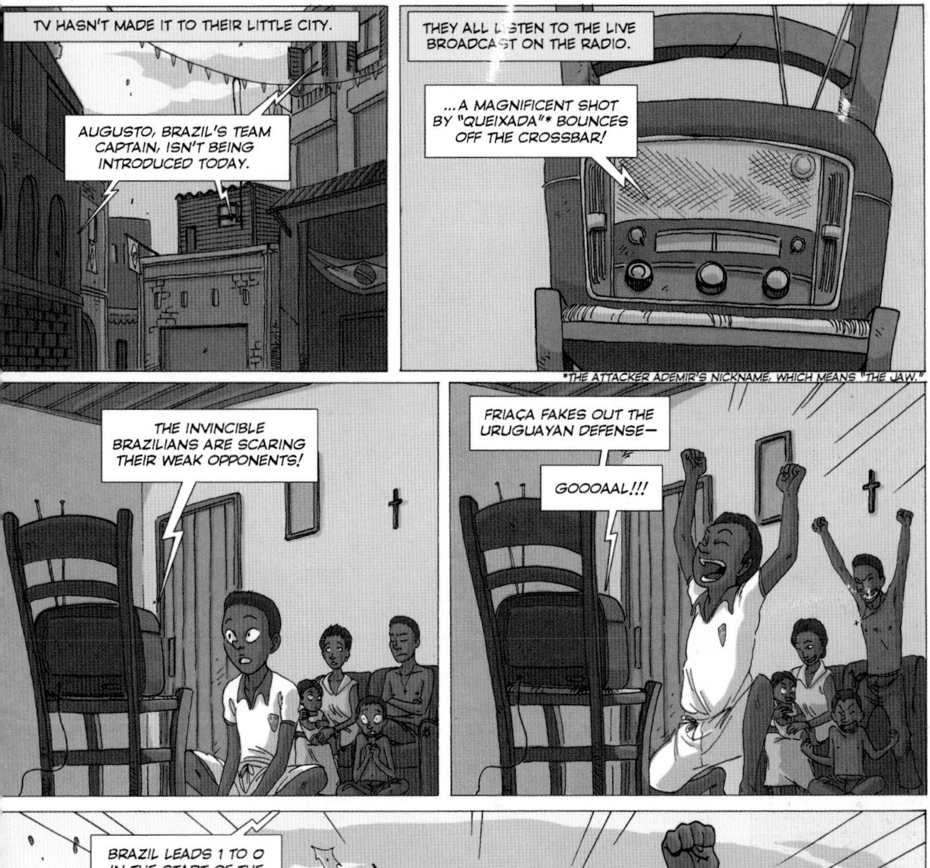
TV HASN'T MADE IT TO THEIR LITTLE CITY.
AUGUSTO, BRAZIL'S TEAM CAPTAIN, ISN'T BEING INTRODUCED TODAY.
THEY ALL LISTEN TO THE LIVE BROADCAST ON THE RADIO.
...A MAGNIFICENT SHOT BY "QUEIXADA"* BOUNCES OFF THE CROSSBAR!
THE INVINCIBLE BRAZILIANS ARE SCARING THEIR WEAK OPPONENTS!
FRIAÇA FAKES OUT THE URUGUAYAN DEFENSE—
GOOOAAL!!!
BRAZIL LEADS 1 TO 0 IN THE START OF THE SECOND HALF!
POW!
POW!
POW!
BUT—GOAL FROM URUGUAY!!!
*THE ATTACKER ADEMIR'S NICKNAME, WHICH MEANS "THE JAW."

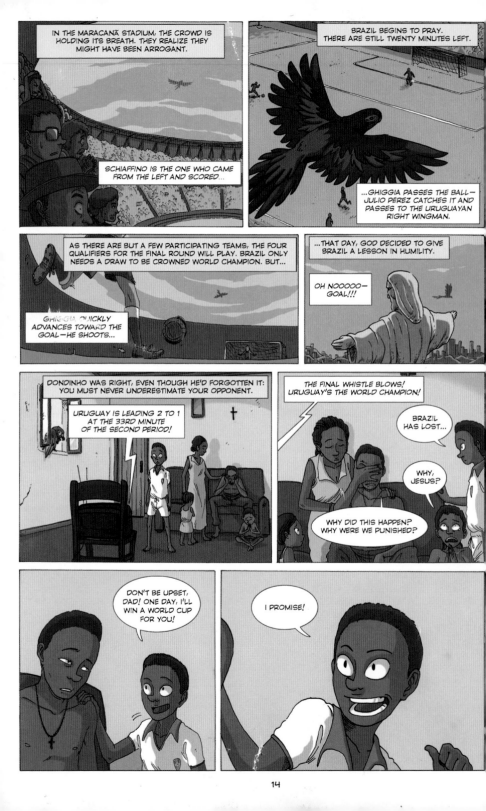

Chapter 2
When Dico Becomes Pelé

"I don't want to be famous. I don't want to be a great player.
I just want to be like my father." —Pelé, 1952

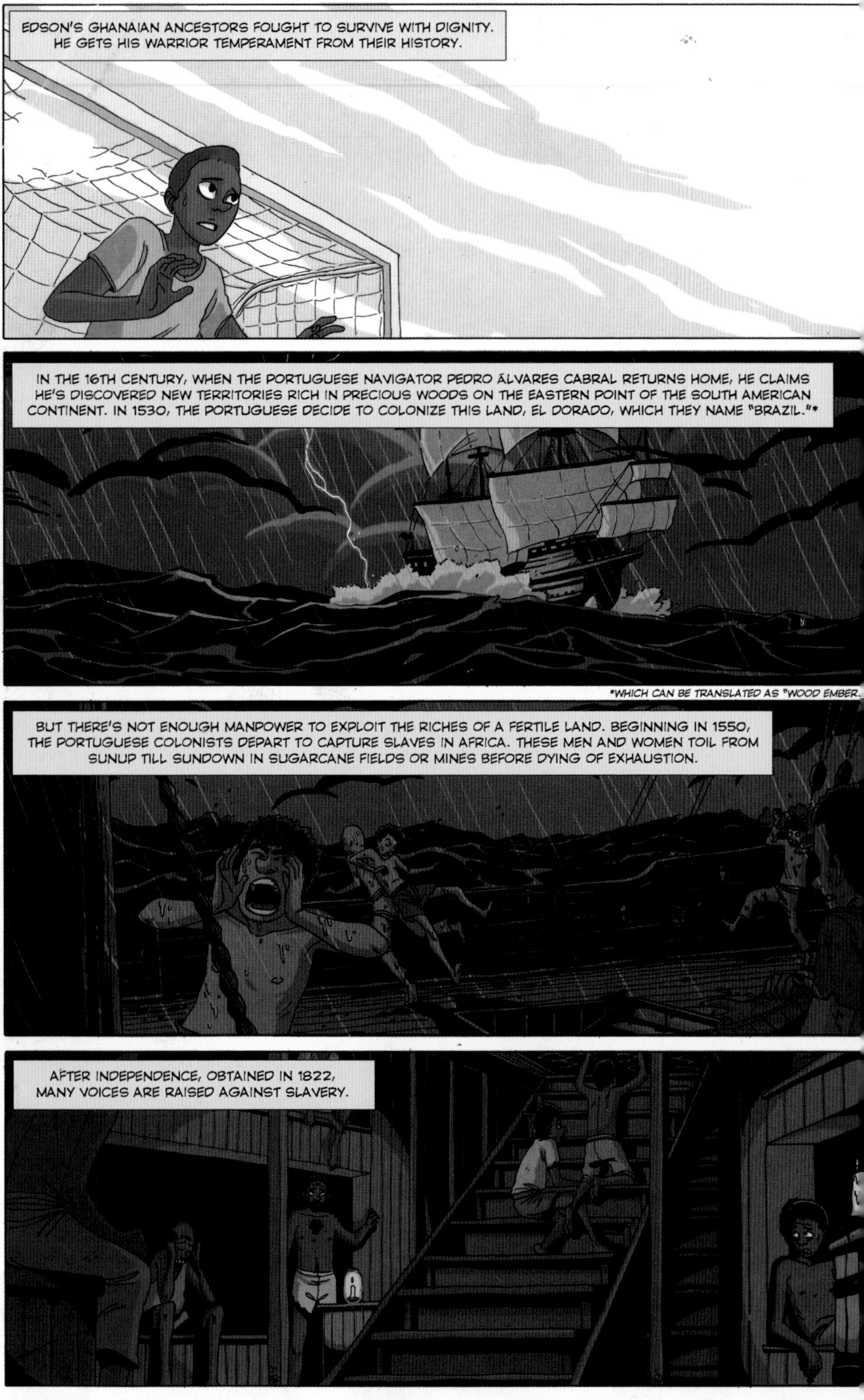
EDSON'S GHANAIAN ANCESTORS FOUGHT TO SURVIVE WITH DIGNITY. HE GETS HIS WARRIOR TEMPERAMENT FROM THEIR HISTORY.
IN THE 16TH CENTURY, WHEN THE PORTUGUESE NAVIGATOR PEDRO ÁLVARES CABRAL RETURNS HOME, HE CLAIMS HE'S DISCOVERED NEW TERRITORIES RICH IN PRECIOUS WOODS ON THE EASTERN POINT OF THE SOUTH AMERICAN CONTINENT. IN 1530, THE PORTUGUESE DECIDE TO COLONIZE THIS LAND, EL DORADO, WHICH THEY NAME "BRAZIL."*
*WHICH CAN BE TRANSLATED AS "WOOD EMBER.
BUT THERE'S NOT ENOUGH MANPOWER TO EXPLOIT THE RICHES OF A FERTILE LAND. BEGINNING IN 1550, THE PORTUGUESE COLONISTS DEPART TO CAPTURE SLAVES IN AFRICA. THESE MEN AND WOMEN TOIL FROM SUNUP TILL SUNDOWN IN SUGARCANE FIELDS OR MINES BEFORE DYING OF EXHAUSTION.
AFTER INDEPENDENCE, OBTAINED IN 1822, MANY VOICES ARE RAISED AGAINST SLAVERY.

*BILÊ WAS THE NICKNAME FOR THE SEMIPROFESSIONAL GOALKEEPER OF THE BAURU ATLÉTICO CLUBE.

17

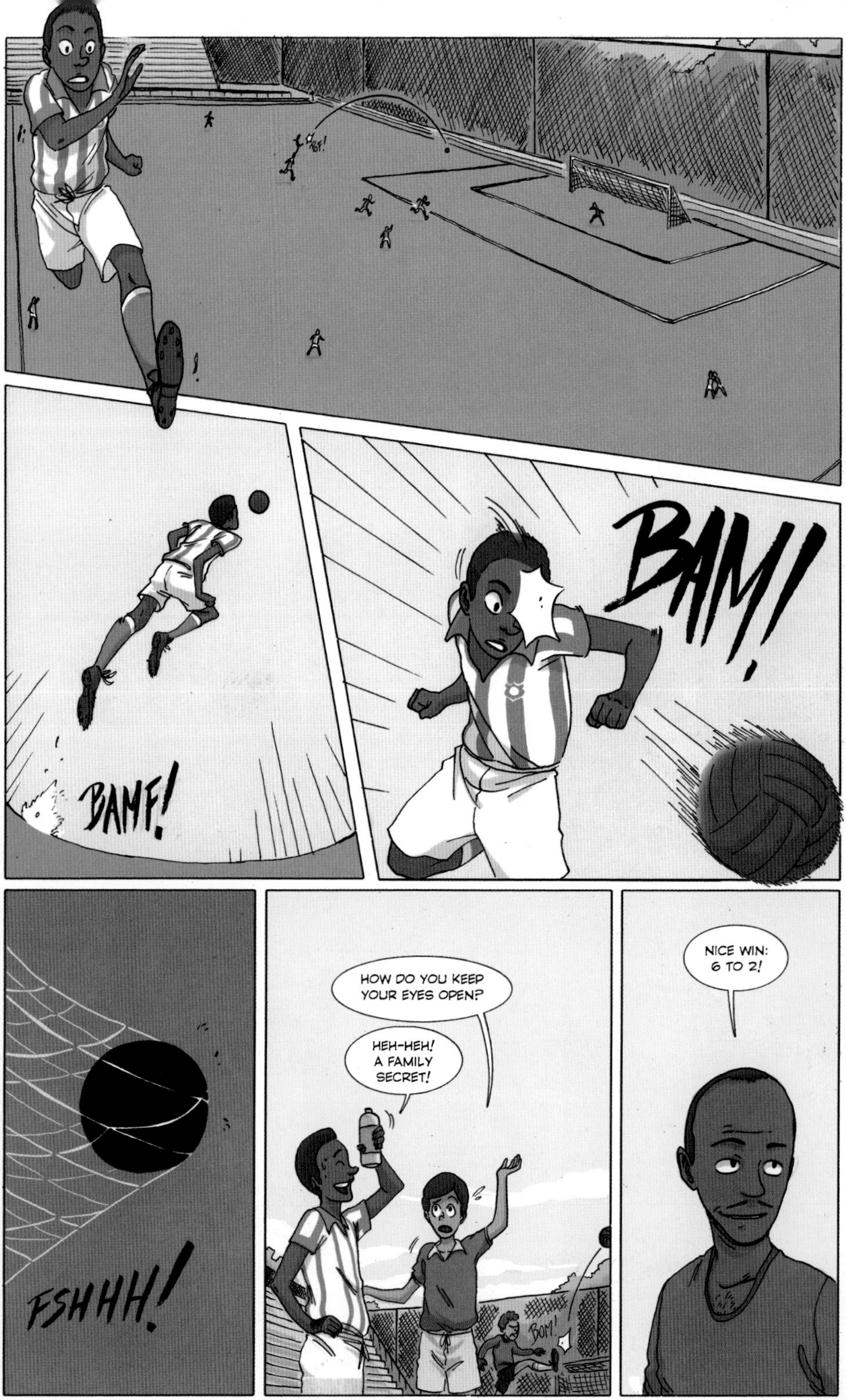
BOF!
BAMF!
BAM!
FSHHH!
HOW DO YOU KEEP YOUR EYES OPEN?
HEH-HEH! A FAMILY SECRET!
BOM!
NICE WIN: 6 TO 2!

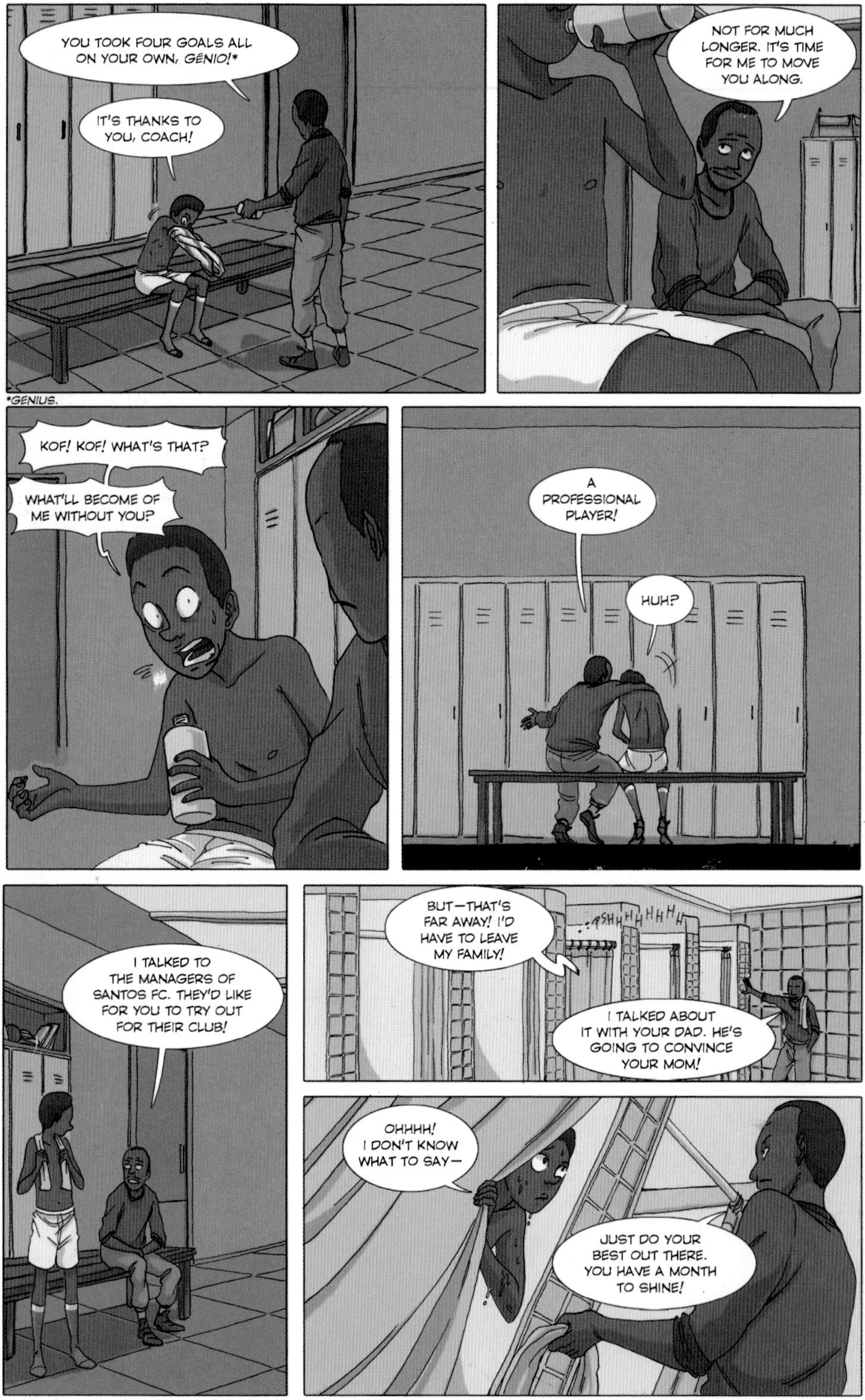
YOU TOOK FOUR GOALS ALL ON YOUR OWN, *GÊNIO*!*
IT'S THANKS TO YOU, COACH!
NOT FOR MUCH LONGER. IT'S TIME FOR ME TO MOVE YOU ALONG.
KOF! KOF! WHAT'S THAT?
WHAT'LL BECOME OF ME WITHOUT YOU?
A PROFESSIONAL PLAYER!
HUH?
I TALKED TO THE MANAGERS OF SANTOS FC. THEY'D LIKE FOR YOU TO TRY OUT FOR THEIR CLUB!
BUT—THAT'S FAR AWAY! I'D HAVE TO LEAVE MY FAMILY!
PSHHHHHHHHH
I TALKED ABOUT IT WITH YOUR DAD. HE'S GOING TO CONVINCE YOUR MOM!
OHHHH! I DON'T KNOW WHAT TO SAY—
JUST DO YOUR BEST OUT THERE. YOU HAVE A MONTH TO SHINE!

*GENIUS.

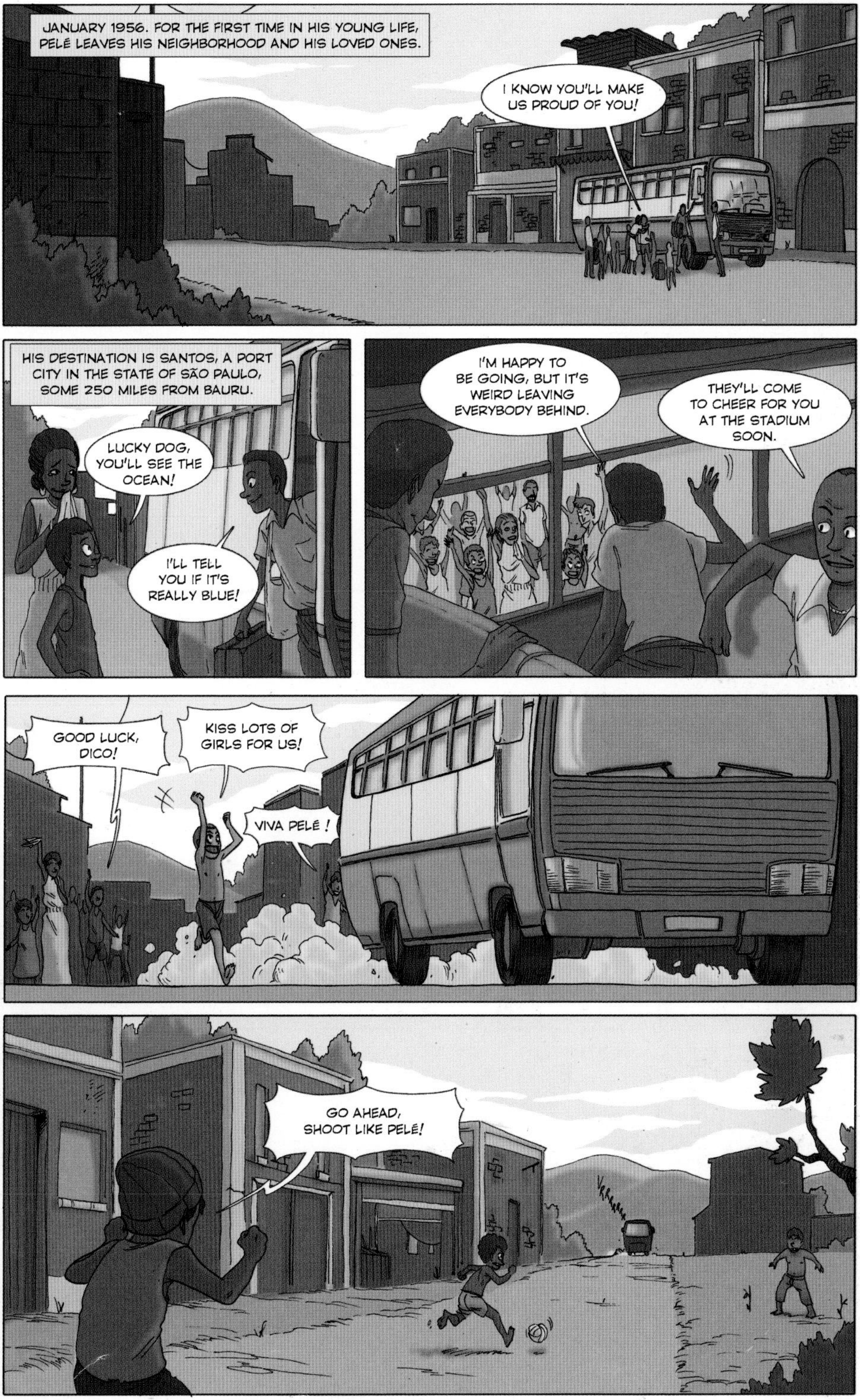
JANUARY 1956. FOR THE FIRST TIME IN HIS YOUNG LIFE, PELÉ LEAVES HIS NEIGHBORHOOD AND HIS LOVED ONES.
I KNOW YOU'LL MAKE US PROUD OF YOU!
HIS DESTINATION IS SANTOS, A PORT CITY IN THE STATE OF SÃO PAULO, SOME 250 MILES FROM BAURU.
LUCKY DOG, YOU'LL SEE THE OCEAN!
I'LL TELL YOU IF IT'S REALLY BLUE!
I'M HAPPY TO BE GOING, BUT IT'S WEIRD LEAVING EVERYBODY BEHIND.
THEY'LL COME TO CHEER FOR YOU AT THE STADIUM SOON.
GOOD LUCK, DICO!
KISS LOTS OF GIRLS FOR US!
VIVA PELÉ !
GO AHEAD, SHOOT LIKE PELÉ!

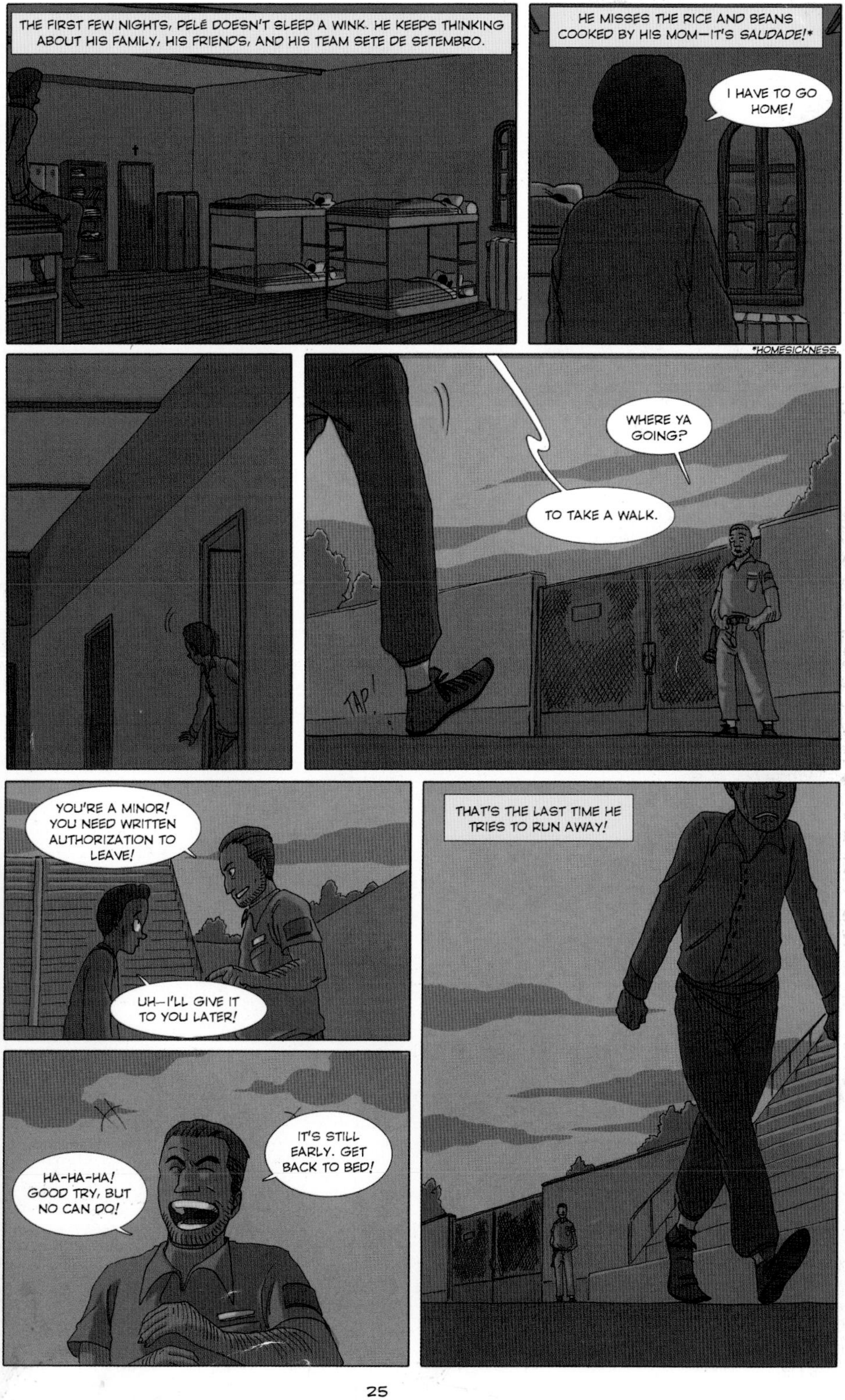
THE FIRST FEW NIGHTS, PELÉ DOESN'T SLEEP A WINK. HE KEEPS THINKING ABOUT HIS FAMILY, HIS FRIENDS, AND HIS TEAM SETE DE SETEMBRO.
HE MISSES THE RICE AND BEANS COOKED BY HIS MOM—IT'S *SAUDADE!**
I HAVE TO GO HOME!
*HOMESICKNESS.
WHERE YA GOING?
TO TAKE A WALK.
TAP!
YOU'RE A MINOR! YOU NEED WRITTEN AUTHORIZATION TO LEAVE!
UH—I'LL GIVE IT TO YOU LATER!
HA-HA-HA! GOOD TRY, BUT NO CAN DO!
IT'S STILL EARLY. GET BACK TO BED!
THAT'S THE LAST TIME HE TRIES TO RUN AWAY!

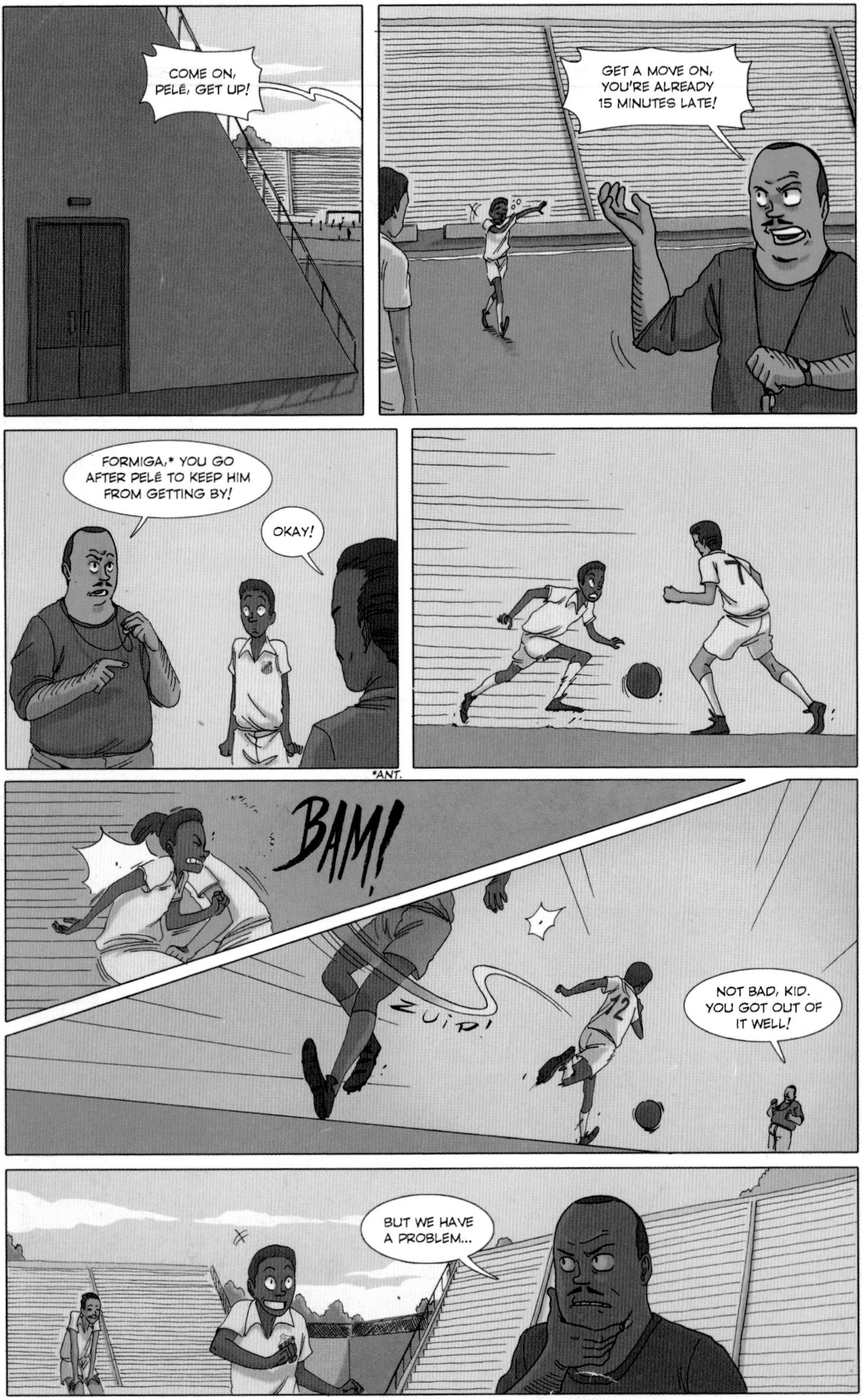
COME ON, PELÉ, GET UP!
GET A MOVE ON, YOU'RE ALREADY 15 MINUTES LATE!
FORMIGA,* YOU GO AFTER PELÉ TO KEEP HIM FROM GETTING BY!
OKAY!
*ANT.
BAM!
ZUIP!
NOT BAD, KID. YOU GOT OUT OF IT WELL!
BUT WE HAVE A PROBLEM...

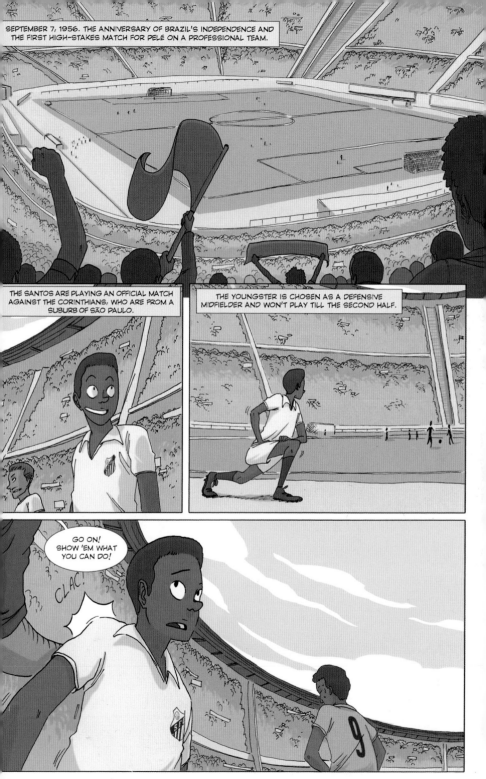

SEPTEMBER 7, 1956. THE ANNIVERSARY OF BRAZIL'S INDEPENDENCE AND THE FIRST HIGH-STAKES MATCH FOR PELÉ ON A PROFESSIONAL TEAM.

THE SANTOS ARE PLAYING AN OFFICIAL MATCH AGAINST THE CORINTHIANS, WHO ARE FROM A SUBURB OF SÃO PAULO.

THE YOUNGSTER IS CHOSEN AS A DEFENSIVE MIDFIELDER AND WON'T PLAY TILL THE SECOND HALF.

GO ON! SHOW 'EM WHAT YOU CAN DO!

CLAC!

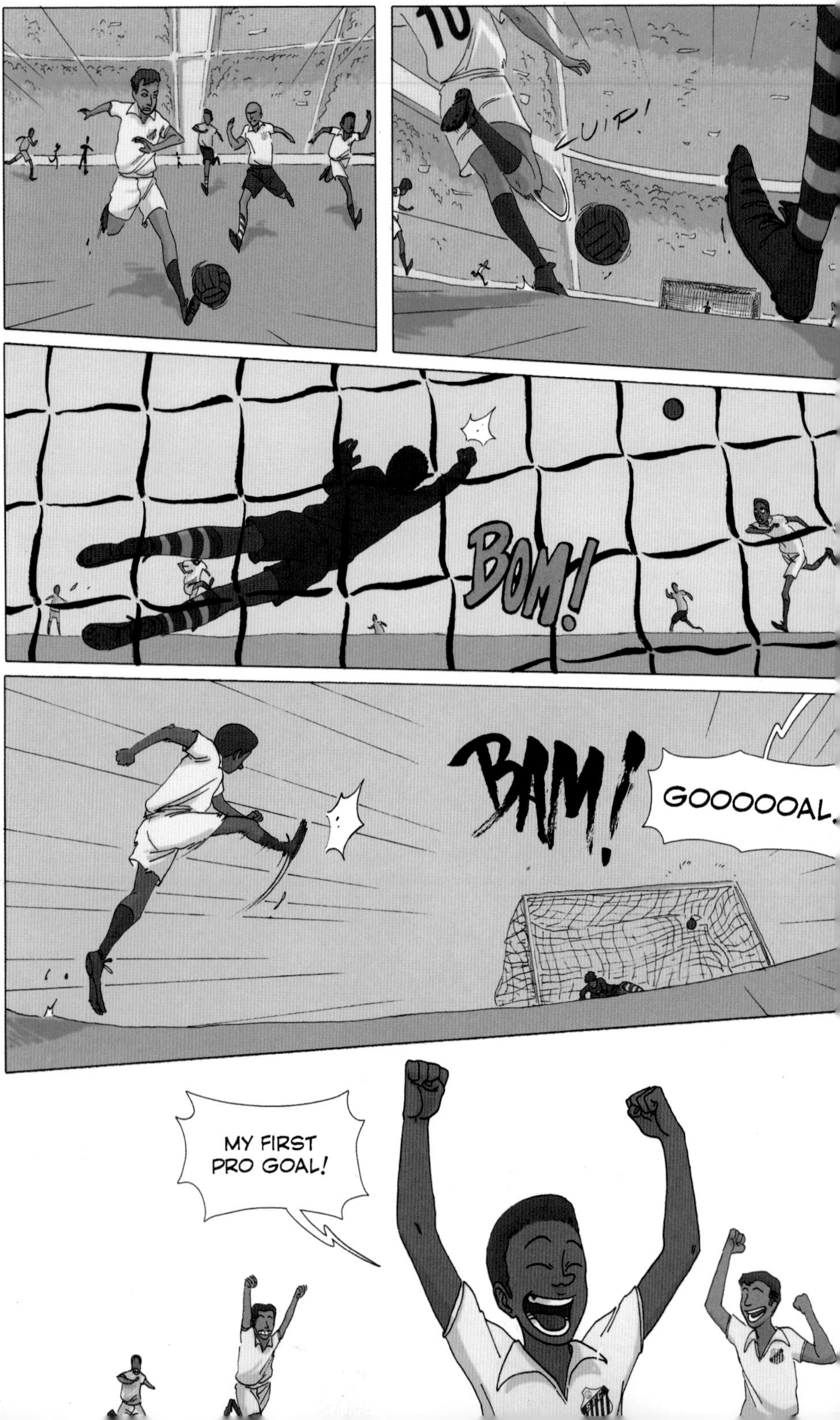
VUIP!
BOM!
BAM!
GOOOOOAL.
MY FIRST PRO GOAL!

Chapter 3
1958, the Birth of a King

"The Santos number 10 jersey was unquestionably mine—
until the arrival of a little black kid with legs as big as matchsticks,
who went down in history by the name of Pelé." —Vasco Vasconcelos

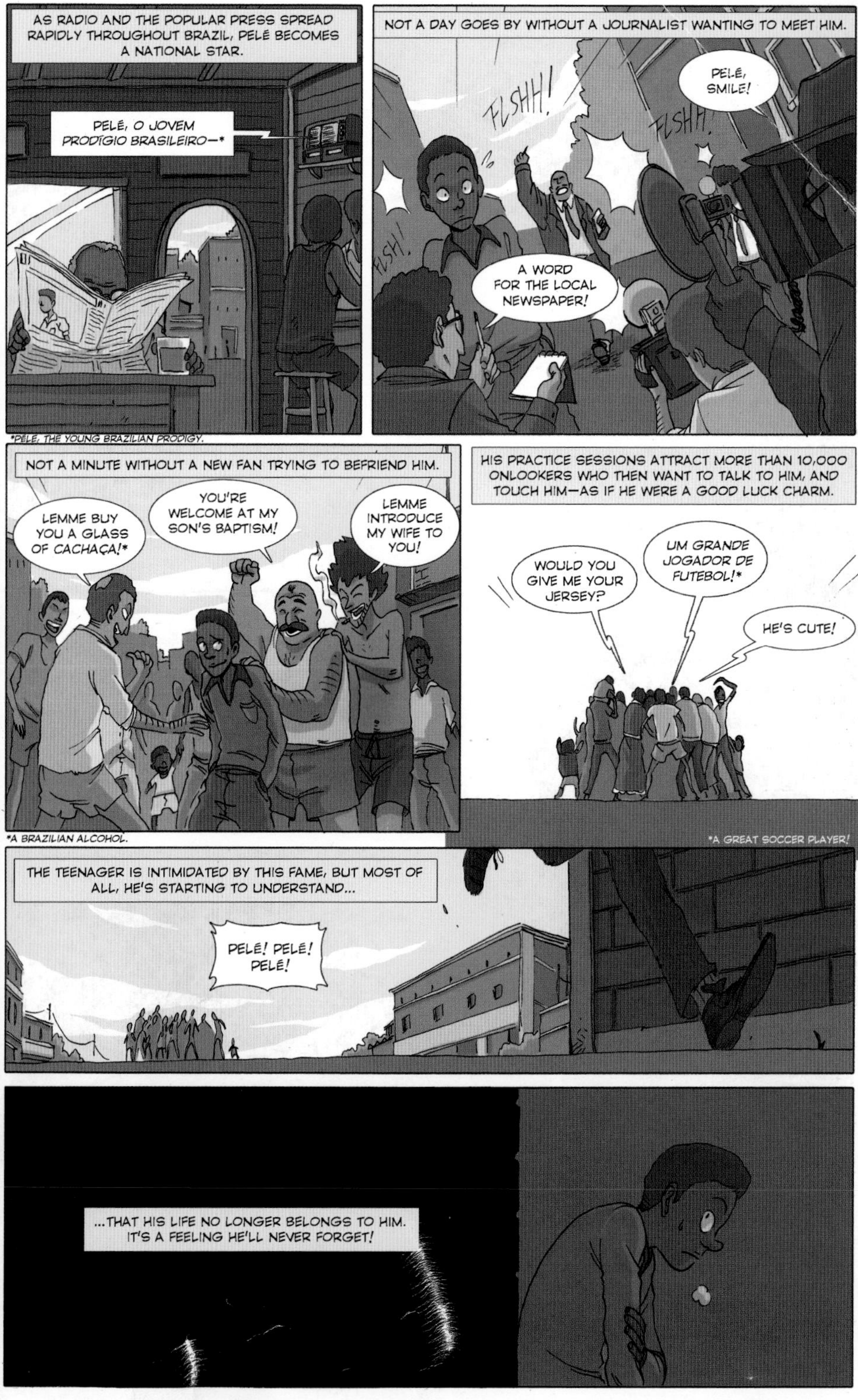
AS RADIO AND THE POPULAR PRESS SPREAD RAPIDLY THROUGHOUT BRAZIL, PELÉ BECOMES A NATIONAL STAR.
PELÉ, O JOVEM PRODÍGIO BRASILEIRO—*
*PELÉ, THE YOUNG BRAZILIAN PRODIGY.
NOT A DAY GOES BY WITHOUT A JOURNALIST WANTING TO MEET HIM.
FLSHH!
PELÉ, SMILE!
FLSHH!
FLSH!
A WORD FOR THE LOCAL NEWSPAPER!
NOT A MINUTE WITHOUT A NEW FAN TRYING TO BEFRIEND HIM.
LEMME BUY YOU A GLASS OF CACHAÇA!*
YOU'RE WELCOME AT MY SON'S BAPTISM!
LEMME INTRODUCE MY WIFE TO YOU!
*A BRAZILIAN ALCOHOL.
HIS PRACTICE SESSIONS ATTRACT MORE THAN 10,000 ONLOOKERS WHO THEN WANT TO TALK TO HIM, AND TOUCH HIM—AS IF HE WERE A GOOD LUCK CHARM.
WOULD YOU GIVE ME YOUR JERSEY?
UM GRANDE JOGADOR DE FUTEBOL!*
HE'S CUTE!
*A GREAT SOCCER PLAYER!
THE TEENAGER IS INTIMIDATED BY THIS FAME, BUT MOST OF ALL, HE'S STARTING TO UNDERSTAND...
PELÉ! PELÉ! PELÉ!
...THAT HIS LIFE NO LONGER BELONGS TO HIM. IT'S A FEELING HE'LL NEVER FORGET!

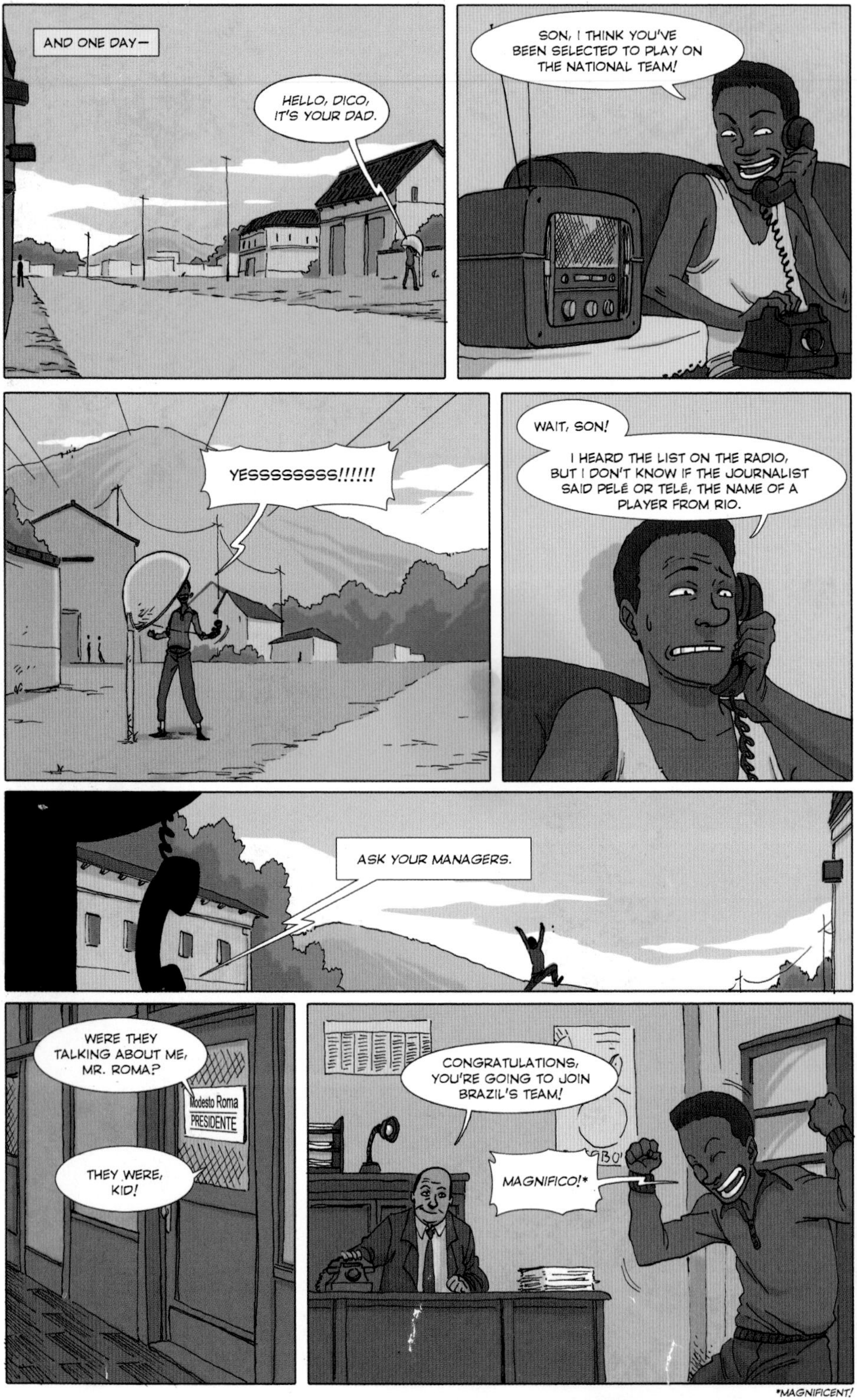
AND ONE DAY—
HELLO, DICO, IT'S YOUR DAD.
SON, I THINK YOU'VE BEEN SELECTED TO PLAY ON THE NATIONAL TEAM!
YESSSSSSSS!!!!!!
WAIT, SON!
I HEARD THE LIST ON THE RADIO, BUT I DON'T KNOW IF THE JOURNALIST SAID PELÉ OR TELÉ, THE NAME OF A PLAYER FROM RIO.
ASK YOUR MANAGERS.
WERE THEY TALKING ABOUT ME, MR. ROMA?
Modesto Roma
PRESIDENTE
THEY WERE, KID!
CONGRATULATIONS, YOU'RE GOING TO JOIN BRAZIL'S TEAM!
MAGNIFICO!*

*MAGNIFICENT!

35

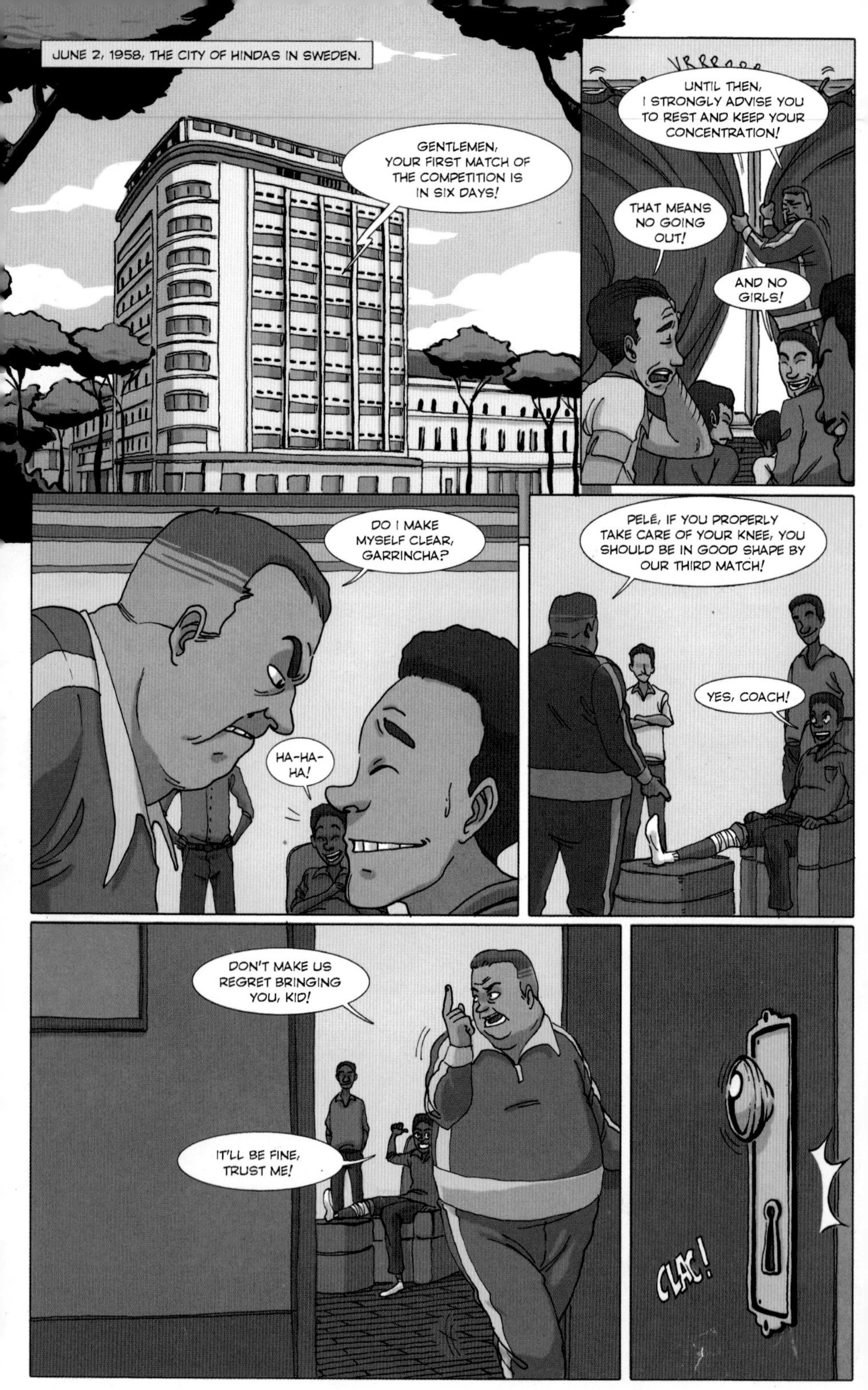
JUNE 2, 1958, THE CITY OF HINDAS IN SWEDEN.
GENTLEMEN, YOUR FIRST MATCH OF THE COMPETITION IS IN SIX DAYS!
UNTIL THEN, I STRONGLY ADVISE YOU TO REST AND KEEP YOUR CONCENTRATION!
THAT MEANS NO GOING OUT!
AND NO GIRLS!
DO I MAKE MYSELF CLEAR, GARRINCHA?
HA-HA-HA!
PELÉ, IF YOU PROPERLY TAKE CARE OF YOUR KNEE, YOU SHOULD BE IN GOOD SHAPE BY OUR THIRD MATCH!
YES, COACH!
DON'T MAKE US REGRET BRINGING YOU, KID!
IT'LL BE FINE, TRUST ME!
CLAC!

39

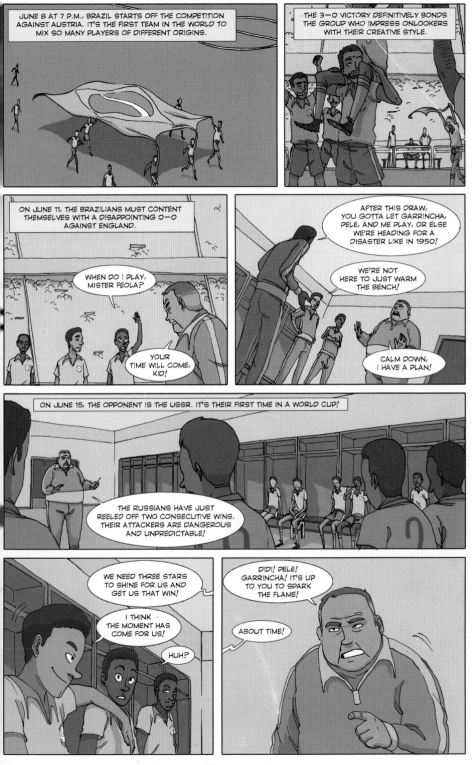

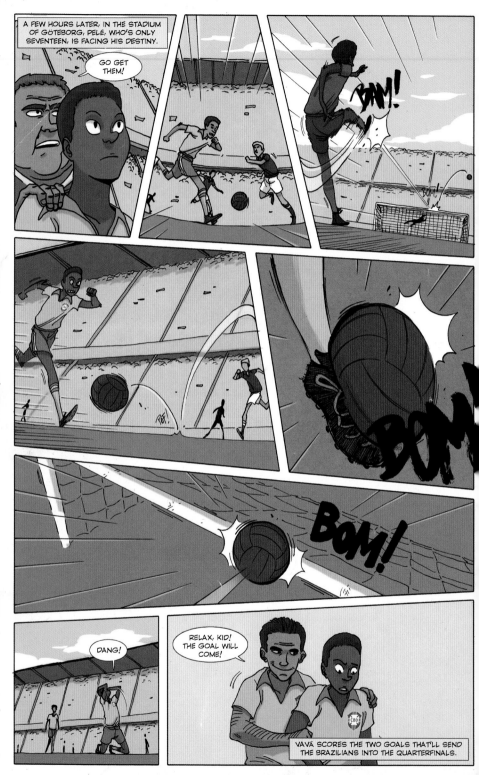

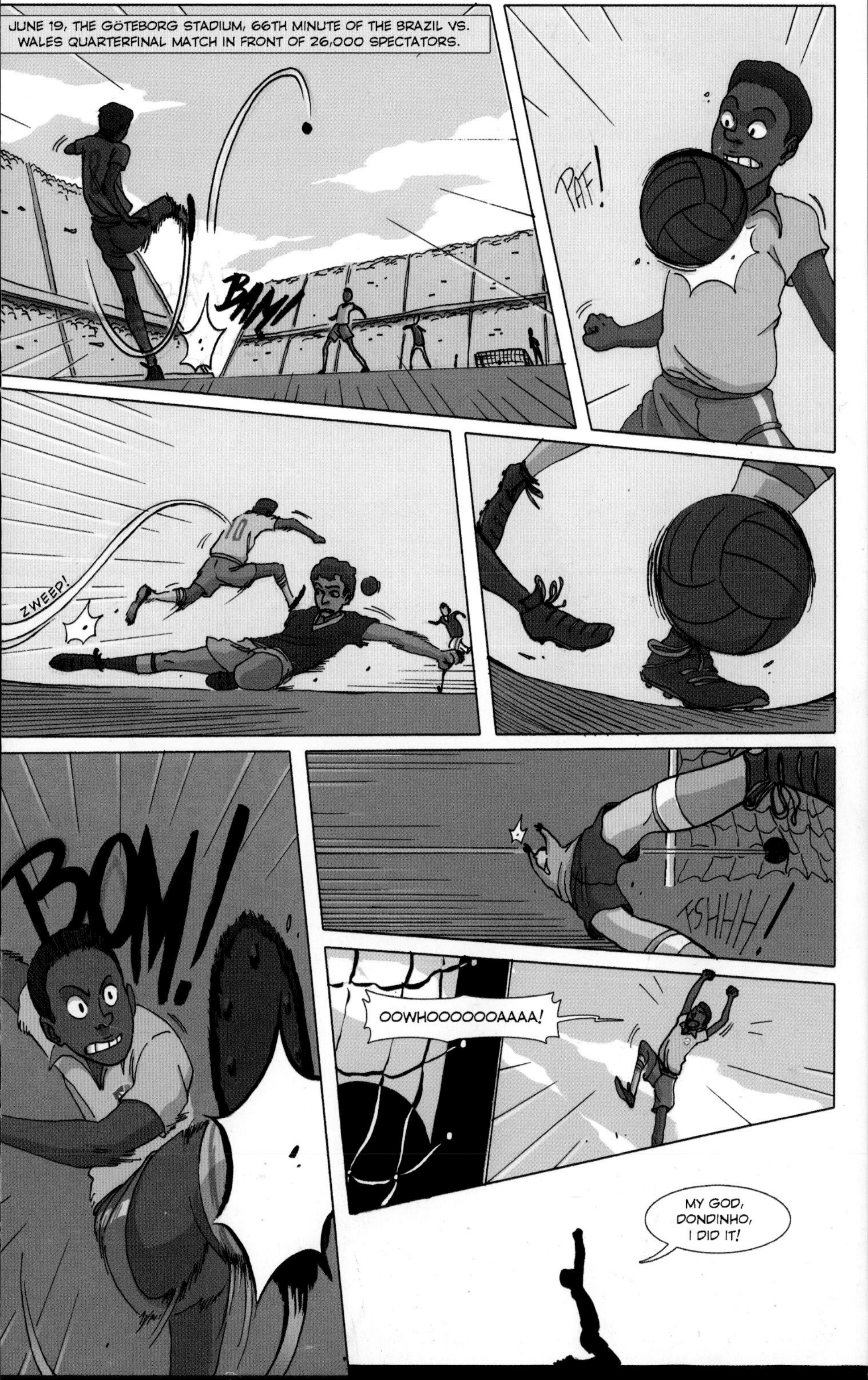
JUNE 19, THE GÖTEBORG STADIUM, 66TH MINUTE OF THE BRAZIL VS. WALES QUARTERFINAL MATCH IN FRONT OF 26,000 SPECTATORS.
BAM!
PAF!
ZWEEP!
BOM!
TSHHH!
OOWHOOOOOOAAAA!
MY GOD, DONDINHO, I DID IT!

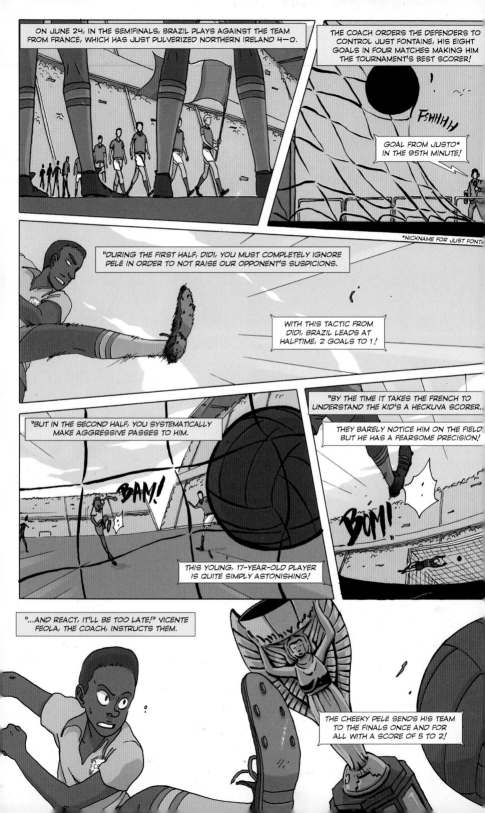

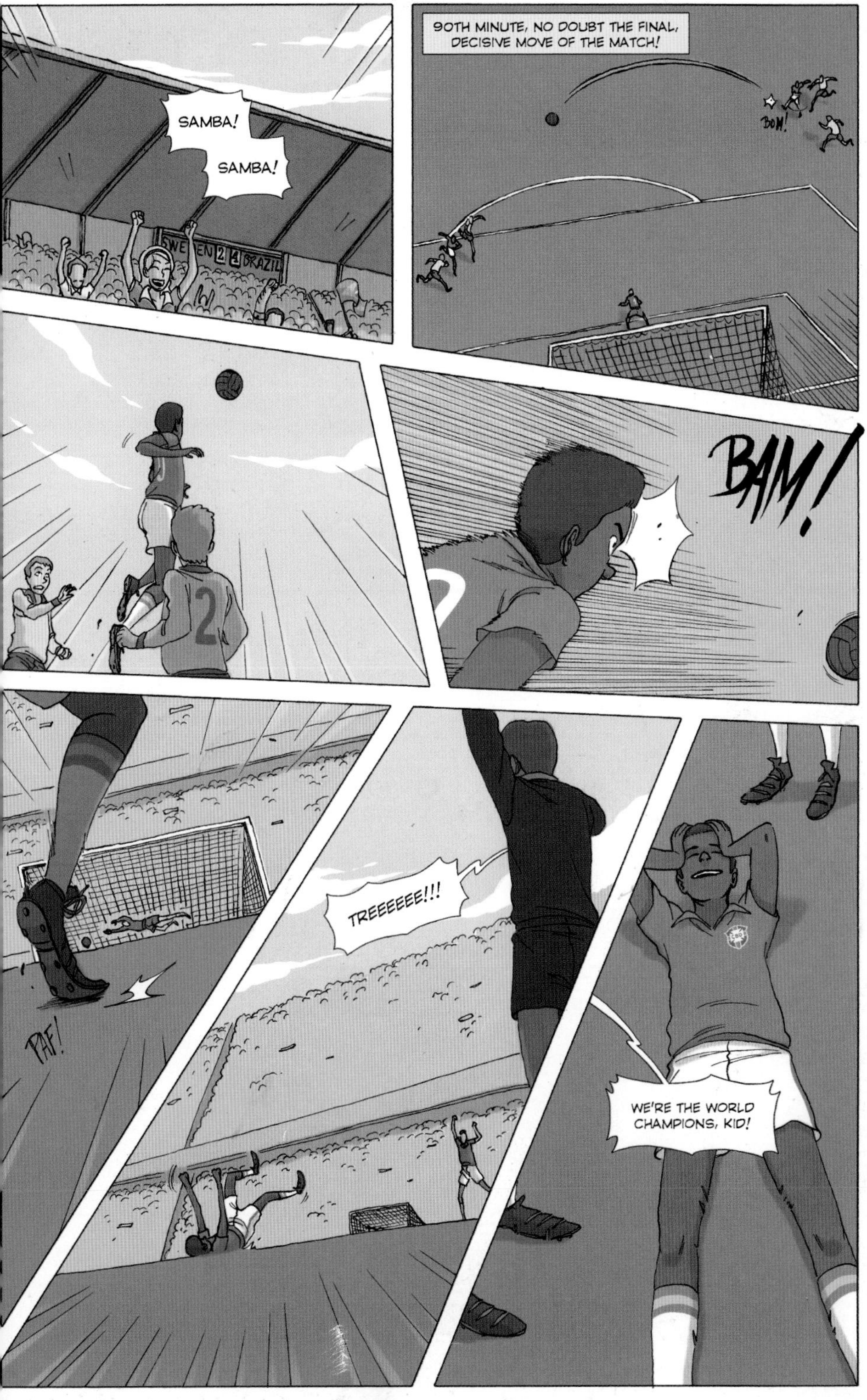
SAMBA!
SAMBA!
SWEDEN 2 4 BRAZIL
90TH MINUTE, NO DOUBT THE FINAL, DECISIVE MOVE OF THE MATCH!
BOM!
BAM!
PAF!
TREEEEEE!!!
WE'RE THE WORLD CHAMPIONS, KID!

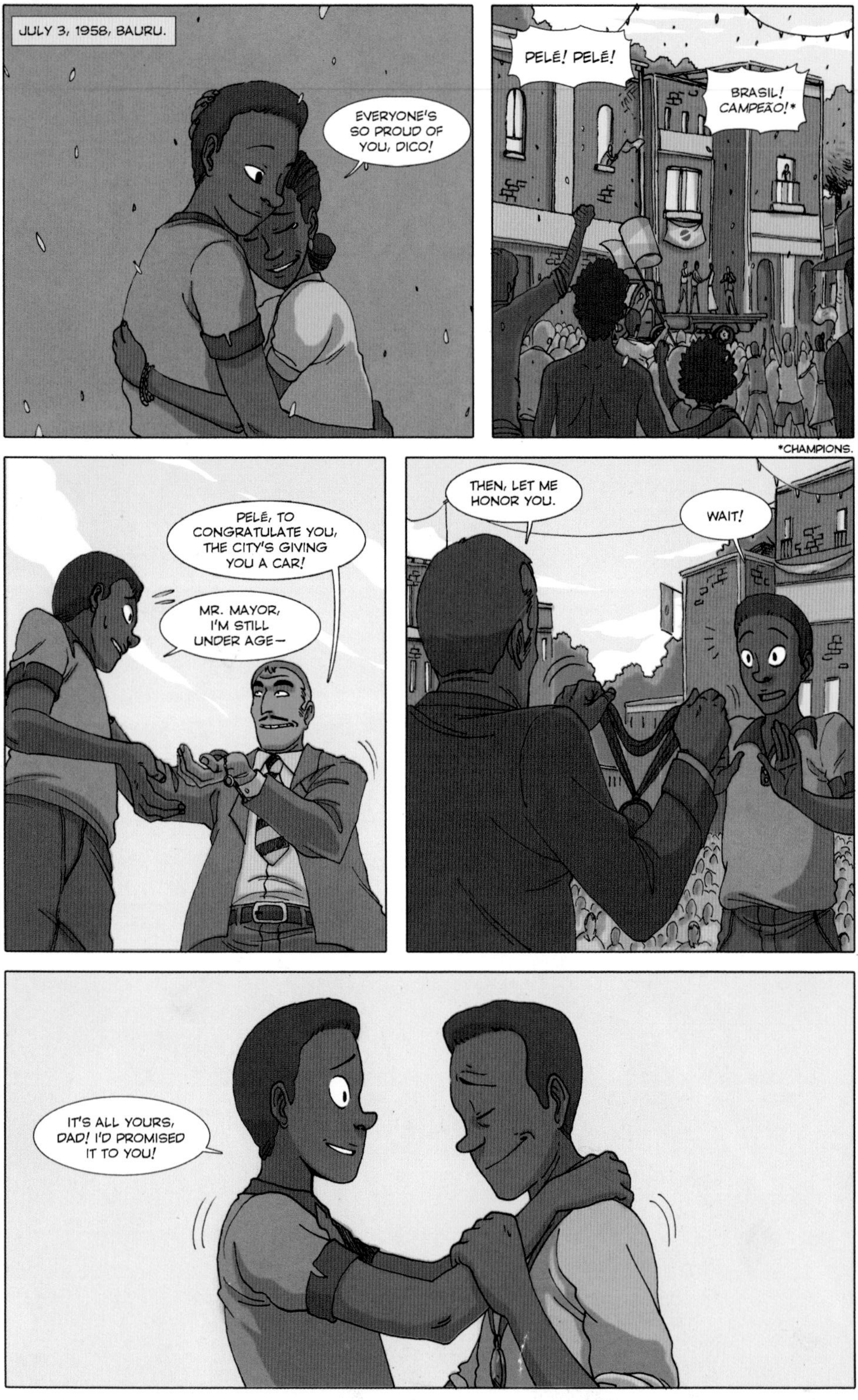
JULY 3, 1958, BAURU.
EVERYONE'S SO PROUD OF YOU, DICO!
PELÉ! PELÉ!
BRASIL! CAMPEÃO!*
*CHAMPIONS.
PELÉ, TO CONGRATULATE YOU, THE CITY'S GIVING YOU A CAR!
MR. MAYOR, I'M STILL UNDER AGE—
THEN, LET ME HONOR YOU.
WAIT!
IT'S ALL YOURS, DAD! I'D PROMISED IT TO YOU!

Chapter 4
A Path Strewn with Rose(s)

"Edson is the person who has feelings, a family, and who works hard. Pelé is the idol." —Pelé, 2003

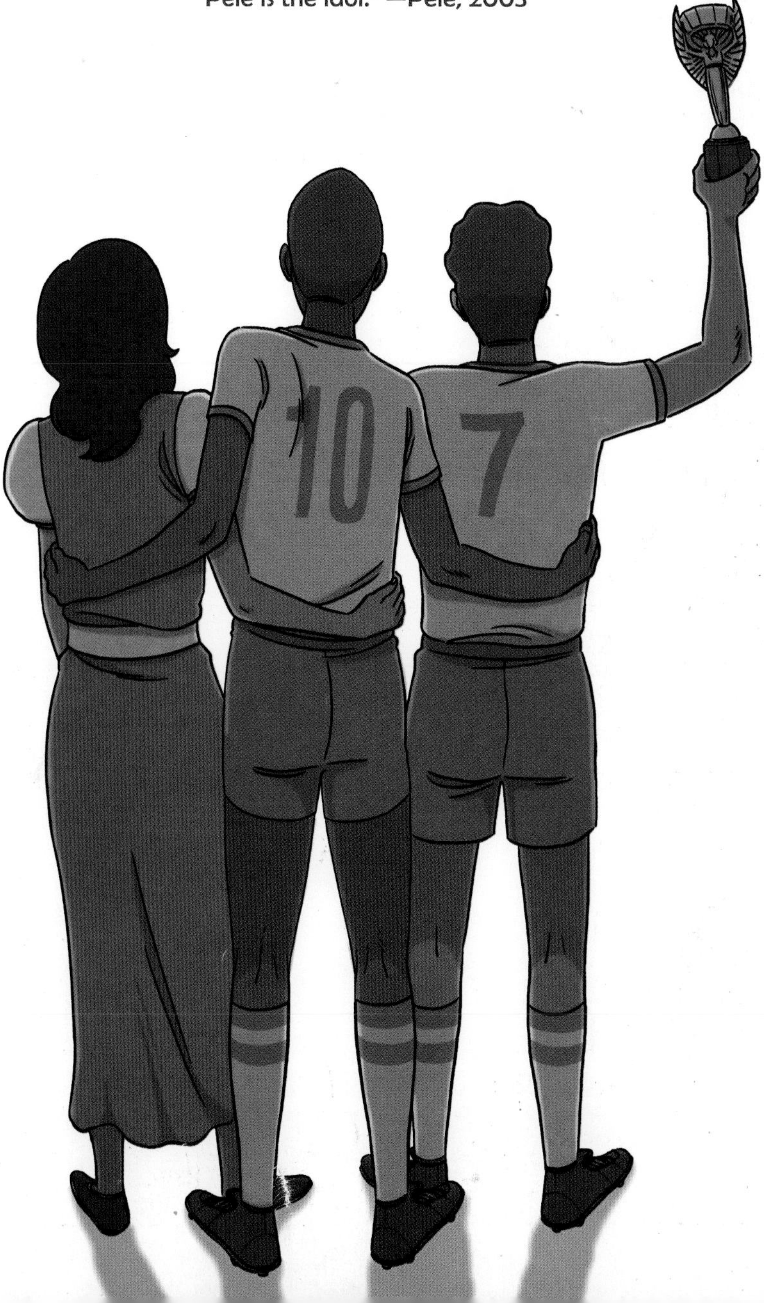

10
7

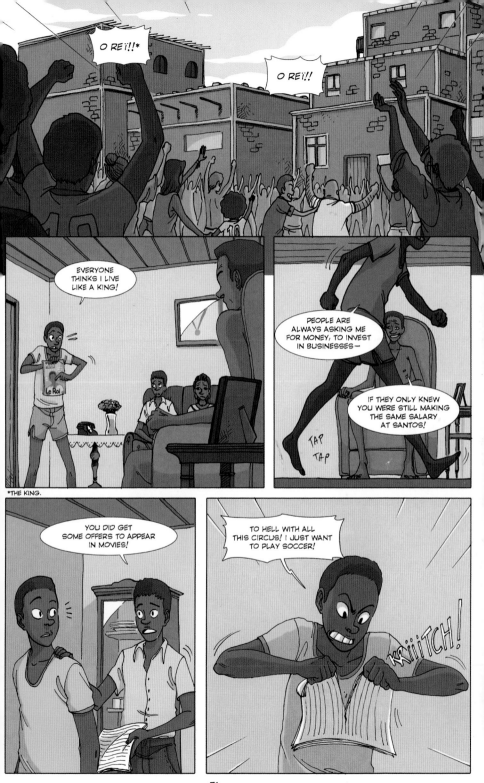

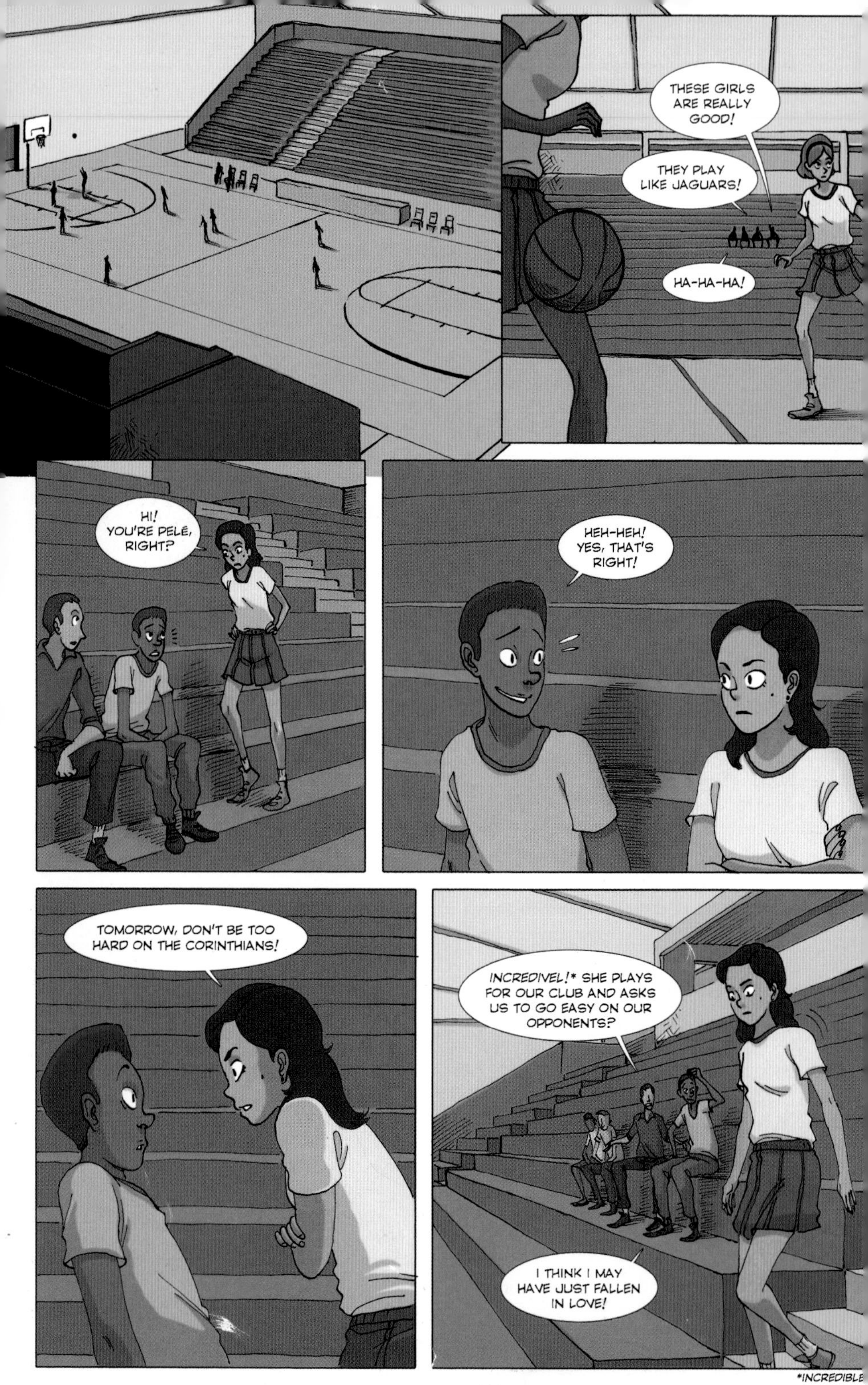
THESE GIRLS ARE REALLY GOOD!
THEY PLAY LIKE JAGUARS!
HA-HA-HA!
HI! YOU'RE PELÉ, RIGHT?
HEH-HEH! YES, THAT'S RIGHT!
TOMORROW, DON'T BE TOO HARD ON THE CORINTHIANS!
INCREDIVEL!* SHE PLAYS FOR OUR CLUB AND ASKS US TO GO EASY ON OUR OPPONENTS?
I THINK I MAY HAVE JUST FALLEN IN LOVE!

*INCREDIBLE

NUMBER 10 ON THE SANTOS COULDN'T TELL YOU WHO WON THE MATCH. HE SPENT THE MAJORITY OF THE 90 MINUTES EYEBALLING THE STANDS SEARCHING FOR HIS MYSTERIOUS BRUNETTE.

PELÉ, YOU'RE PLAYING WITH TWO BUSTED FEET! WHERE'S YOUR MOTIVATION?

NOT HERE!

HE'S DETERMINED TO FIND HER AGAIN! WHEN PELÉ MEETS HER TEAMMATES "BY CHANCE" IN THE STREET, HE DECIDES TO CONDUCT A LITTLE INVESTIGATION.

HER FIRST NAME IS ROSE!

SHE WORKS IN A RECORD STORE DOWNTOWN!

SHE'S A BABY. SHE'S ONLY FOURTEEN!

BUDDY, YOU'RE AS SEXY AS A JK 2000!*

*A FAMOUS BRAZILIAN CAR FROM THE SIXTIES.

DLING!

BOM DIA!* DO YOU REMEMBER ME?

UM—YES.

*HELLO!

55

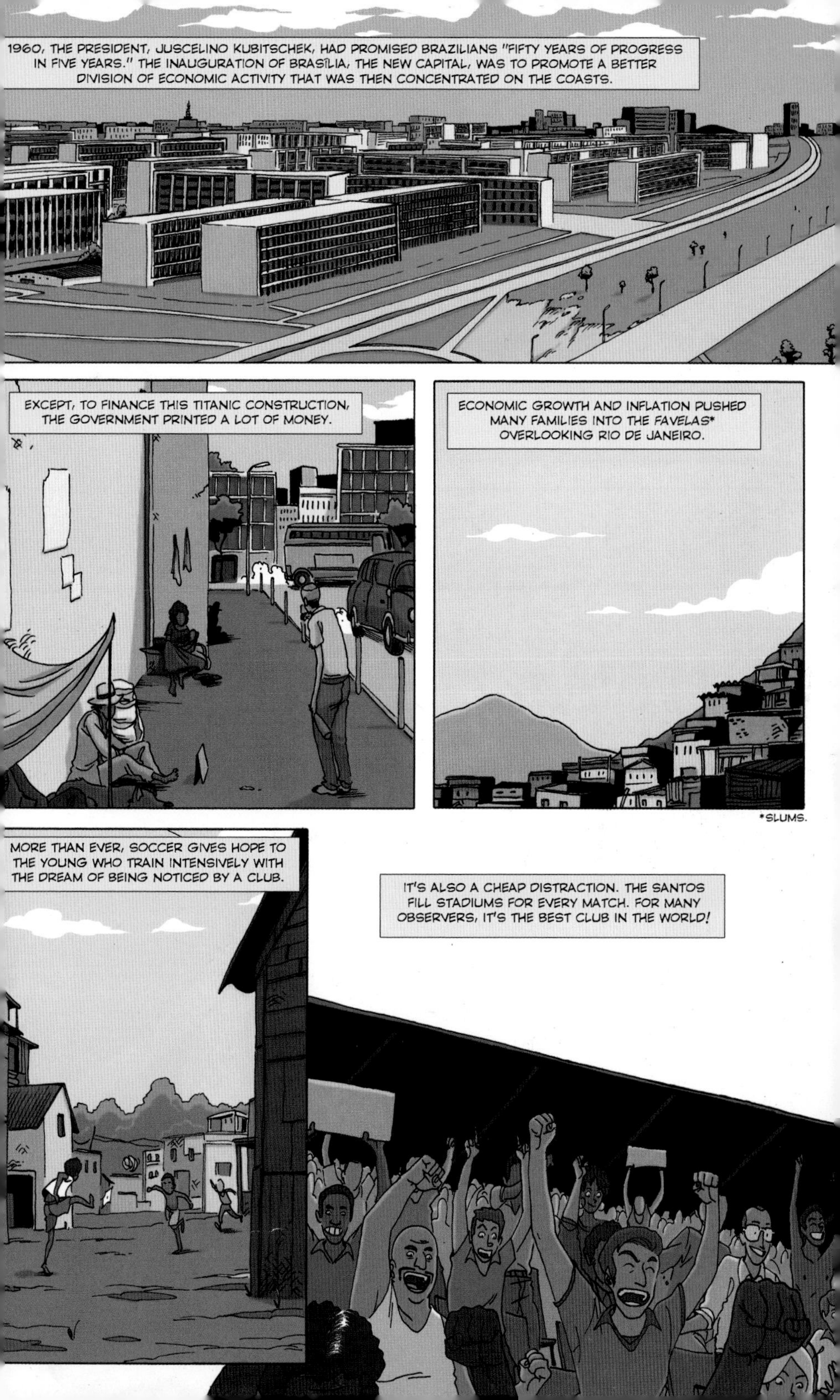
1960, THE PRESIDENT, JUSCELINO KUBITSCHEK, HAD PROMISED BRAZILIANS "FIFTY YEARS OF PROGRESS IN FIVE YEARS." THE INAUGURATION OF BRASÍLIA, THE NEW CAPITAL, WAS TO PROMOTE A BETTER DIVISION OF ECONOMIC ACTIVITY THAT WAS THEN CONCENTRATED ON THE COASTS.
EXCEPT, TO FINANCE THIS TITANIC CONSTRUCTION, THE GOVERNMENT PRINTED A LOT OF MONEY.
ECONOMIC GROWTH AND INFLATION PUSHED MANY FAMILIES INTO THE *FAVELAS** OVERLOOKING RIO DE JANEIRO.
*SLUMS.
MORE THAN EVER, SOCCER GIVES HOPE TO THE YOUNG WHO TRAIN INTENSIVELY WITH THE DREAM OF BEING NOTICED BY A CLUB.
IT'S ALSO A CHEAP DISTRACTION. THE SANTOS FILL STADIUMS FOR EVERY MATCH. FOR MANY OBSERVERS, IT'S THE BEST CLUB IN THE WORLD!

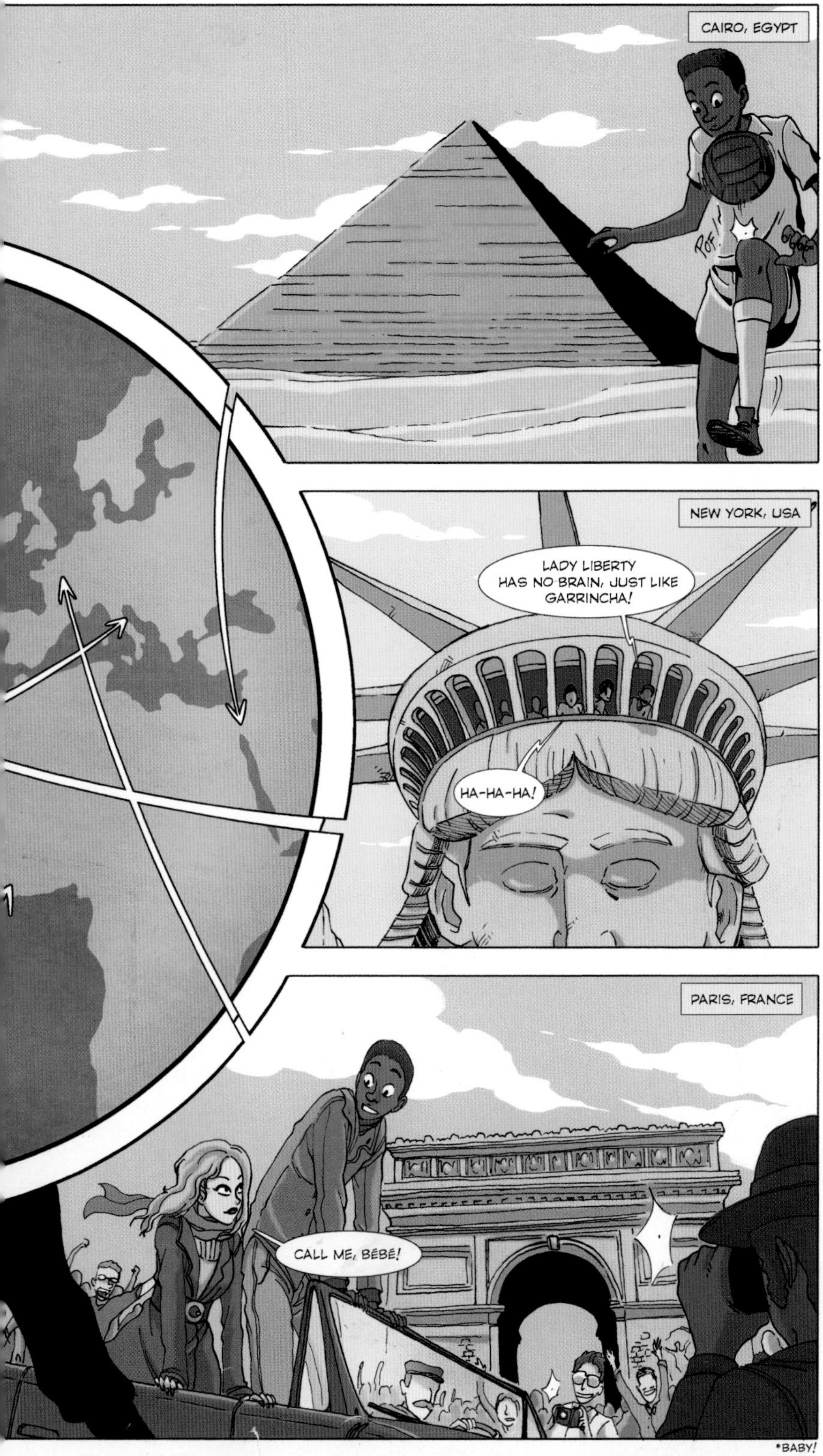
CAIRO, EGYPT
POF!
NEW YORK, USA
LADY LIBERTY HAS NO BRAIN, JUST LIKE GARRINCHA!
HA-HA-HA!
PARIS, FRANCE
CALL ME, BÉBÉ!

*BABY!

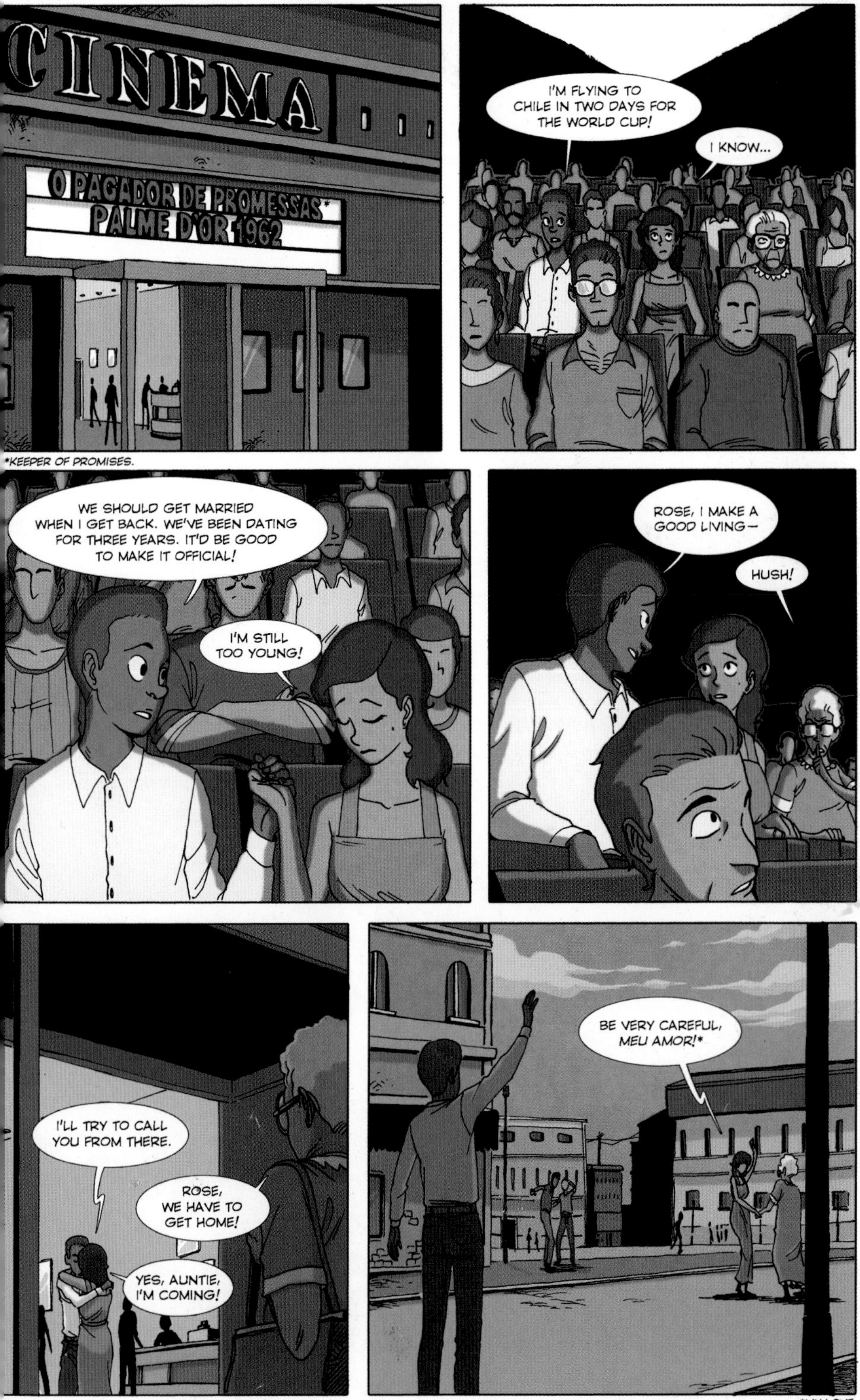
CINEMA
O PAGADOR DE PROMESSAS*
PALME D'OR 1962
I'M FLYING TO CHILE IN TWO DAYS FOR THE WORLD CUP!
I KNOW...
WE SHOULD GET MARRIED WHEN I GET BACK. WE'VE BEEN DATING FOR THREE YEARS. IT'D BE GOOD TO MAKE IT OFFICIAL!
I'M STILL TOO YOUNG!
ROSE, I MAKE A GOOD LIVING—
HUSH!
I'LL TRY TO CALL YOU FROM THERE.
ROSE, WE HAVE TO GET HOME!
YES, AUNTIE, I'M COMING!
BE VERY CAREFUL, MEU AMOR!*

*KEEPER OF PROMISES.

*MY LOVE.

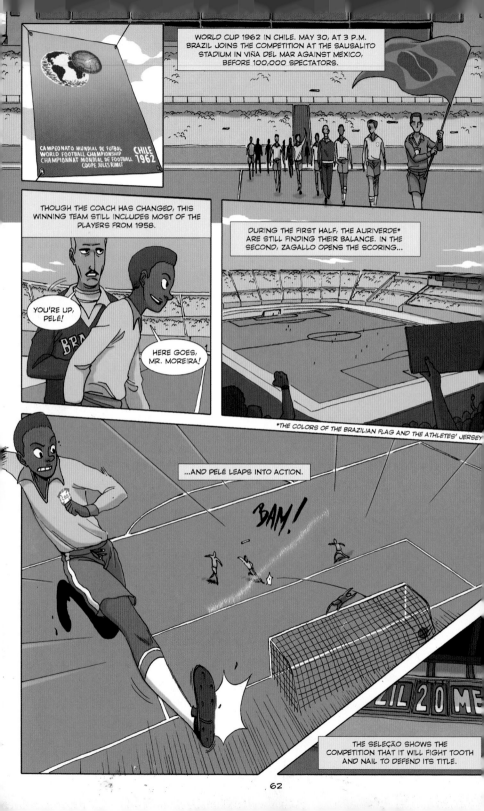

WORLD CUP 1962 IN CHILE. MAY 30, AT 3 P.M. BRAZIL JOINS THE COMPETITION AT THE SAUSALITO STADIUM IN VIÑA DEL MAR AGAINST MEXICO, BEFORE 100,000 SPECTATORS.

CAMPEONATO MUNDIAL DE FUTBOL
WORLD FOOTBALL CHAMPIONSHIP
CHAMPIONNAT MONDIAL DE FOOTBALL
COUPE JULES RIMET
CHILE 1962

THOUGH THE COACH HAS CHANGED, THIS WINNING TEAM STILL INCLUDES MOST OF THE PLAYERS FROM 1958.

YOU'RE UP, PELÉ!

HERE GOES, MR. MOREIRA!

DURING THE FIRST HALF, THE AURIVERDE* ARE STILL FINDING THEIR BALANCE. IN THE SECOND, ZAGALLO OPENS THE SCORING...

*THE COLORS OF THE BRAZILIAN FLAG AND THE ATHLETES' JERSEY

...AND PELÉ LEAPS INTO ACTION.

BAM!

THE SELEÇÃO SHOWS THE COMPETITION THAT IT WILL FIGHT TOOTH AND NAIL TO DEFEND ITS TITLE.

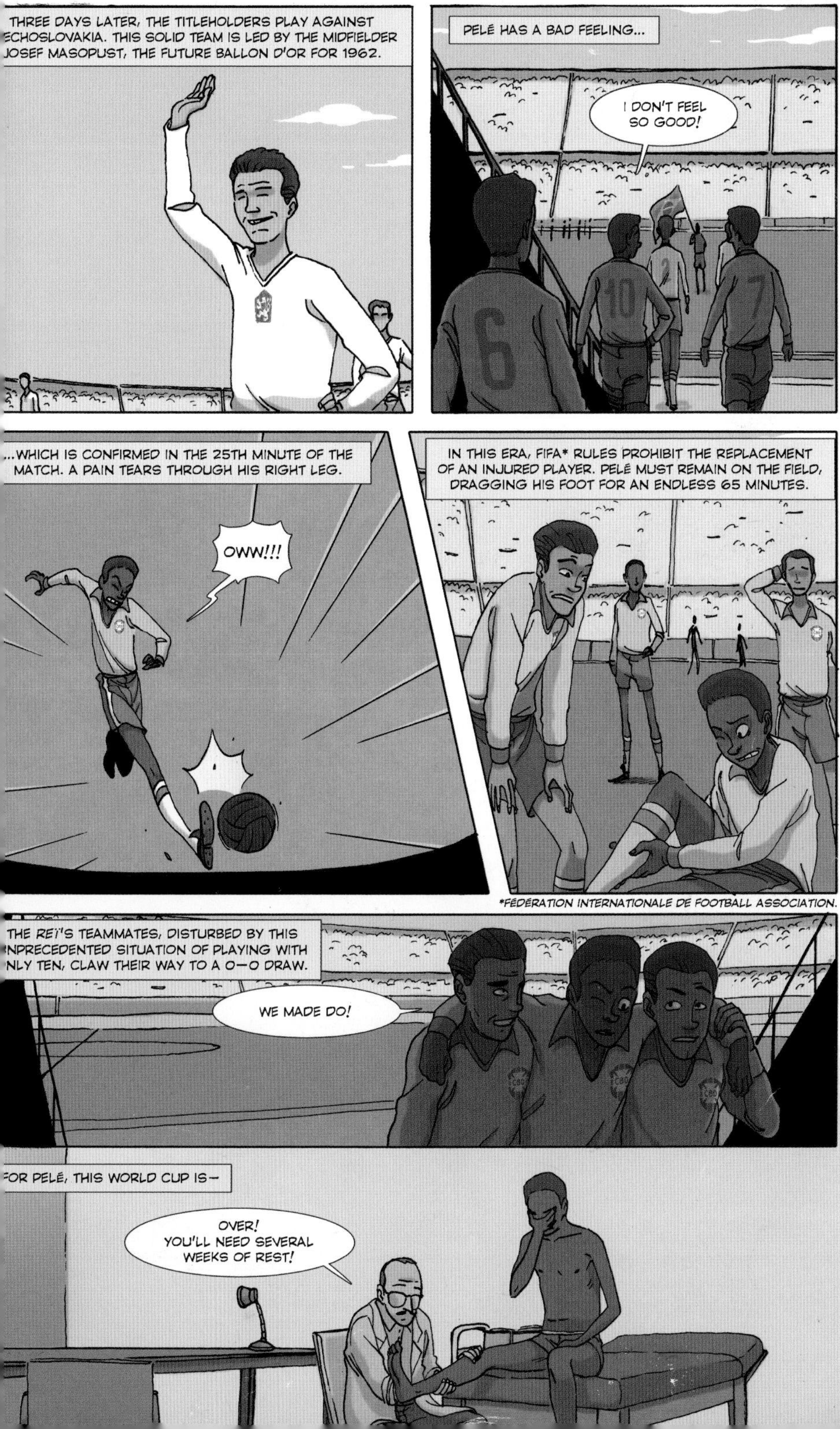
THREE DAYS LATER, THE TITLEHOLDERS PLAY AGAINST ECHOSLOVAKIA. THIS SOLID TEAM IS LED BY THE MIDFIELDER JOSEF MASOPUST, THE FUTURE BALLON D'OR FOR 1962.
PELÉ HAS A BAD FEELING...
I DON'T FEEL SO GOOD!
...WHICH IS CONFIRMED IN THE 25TH MINUTE OF THE MATCH. A PAIN TEARS THROUGH HIS RIGHT LEG.
OWW!!!
IN THIS ERA, FIFA* RULES PROHIBIT THE REPLACEMENT OF AN INJURED PLAYER. PELÉ MUST REMAIN ON THE FIELD, DRAGGING HIS FOOT FOR AN ENDLESS 65 MINUTES.
*FÉDÉRATION INTERNATIONALE DE FOOTBALL ASSOCIATION.
THE *REI*'S TEAMMATES, DISTURBED BY THIS NPRECEDENTED SITUATION OF PLAYING WITH NLY TEN, CLAW THEIR WAY TO A 0–0 DRAW.
WE MADE DO!
OR PELÉ, THIS WORLD CUP IS—
OVER! YOU'LL NEED SEVERAL WEEKS OF REST!

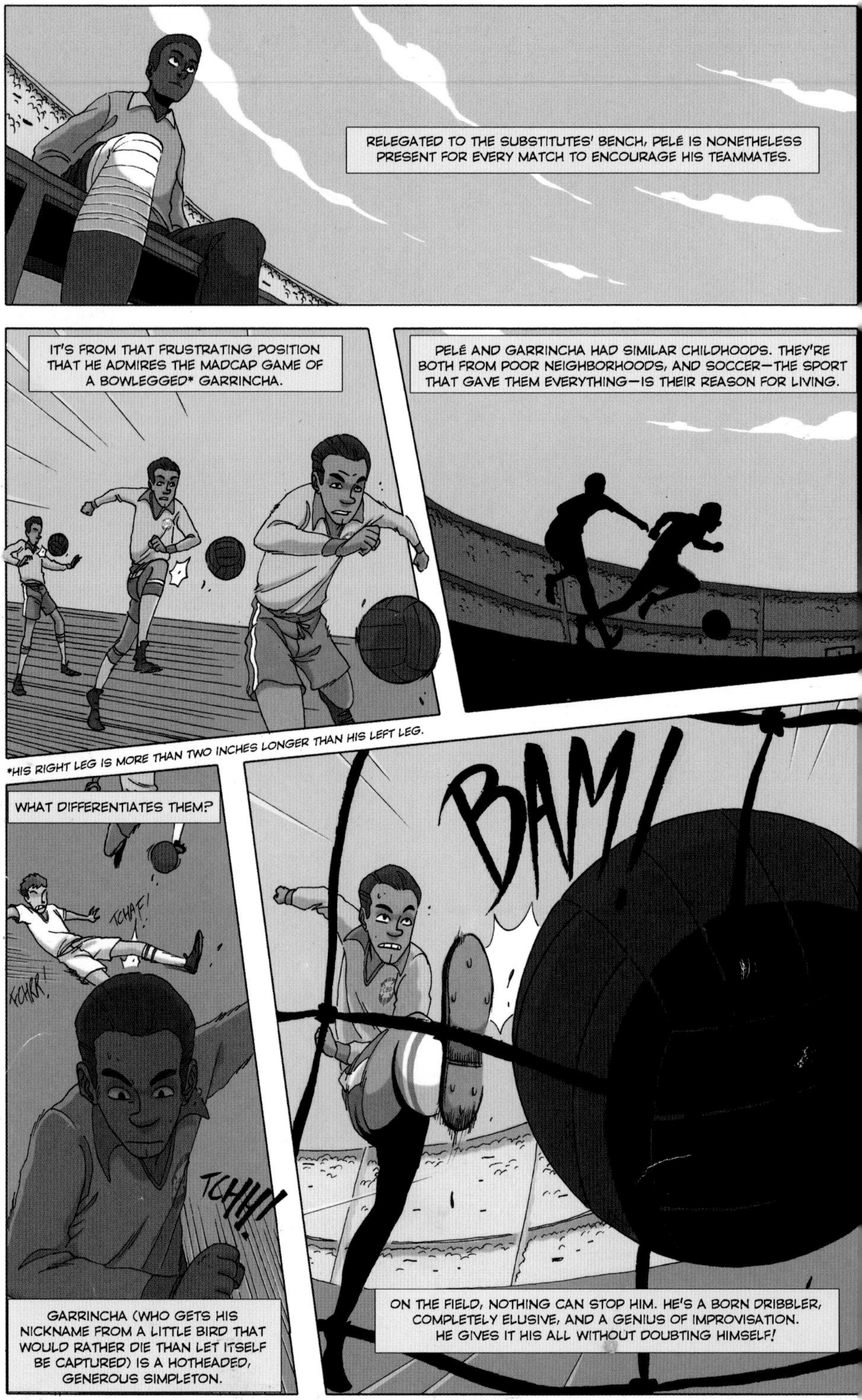

RELEGATED TO THE SUBSTITUTES' BENCH, PELÉ IS NONETHELESS PRESENT FOR EVERY MATCH TO ENCOURAGE HIS TEAMMATES.
IT'S FROM THAT FRUSTRATING POSITION THAT HE ADMIRES THE MADCAP GAME OF A BOWLEGGED* GARRINCHA.
PELÉ AND GARRINCHA HAD SIMILAR CHILDHOODS. THEY'RE BOTH FROM POOR NEIGHBORHOODS, AND SOCCER—THE SPORT THAT GAVE THEM EVERYTHING—IS THEIR REASON FOR LIVING.
*HIS RIGHT LEG IS MORE THAN TWO INCHES LONGER THAN HIS LEFT LEG.
WHAT DIFFERENTIATES THEM?
TCHAF!
TCHRR!
TCHH!
GARRINCHA (WHO GETS HIS NICKNAME FROM A LITTLE BIRD THAT WOULD RATHER DIE THAN LET ITSELF BE CAPTURED) IS A HOTHEADED, GENEROUS SIMPLETON.
BAM!
ON THE FIELD, NOTHING CAN STOP HIM. HE'S A BORN DRIBBLER, COMPLETELY ELUSIVE, AND A GENIUS OF IMPROVISATION. HE GIVES IT HIS ALL WITHOUT DOUBTING HIMSELF!

Chapter 5
O Reï!

"Pelé has extraordinary physical abilities, but he also has intelligence. Few people know he has an IQ above 160. He thinks like a mathematician."
—Professor Julio Mazzei, Pelé's confidant and advisor

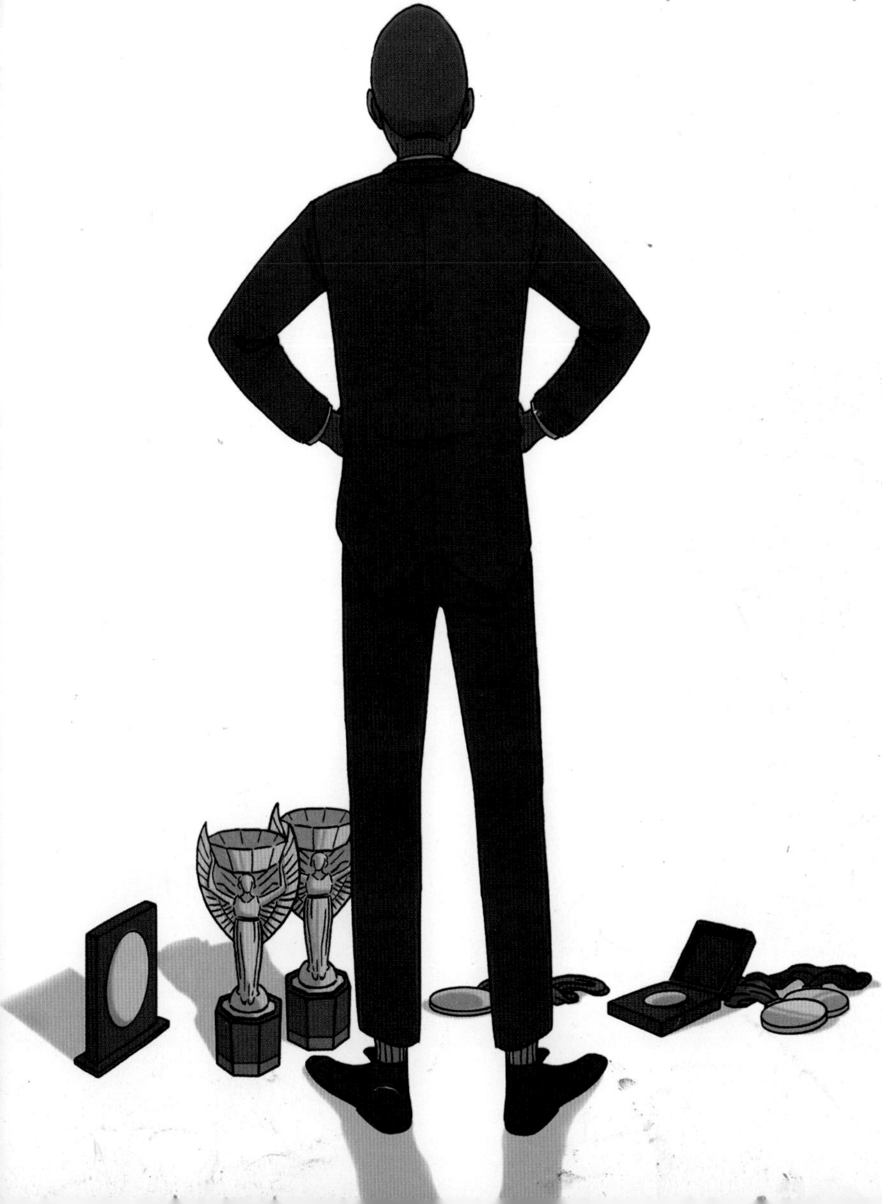

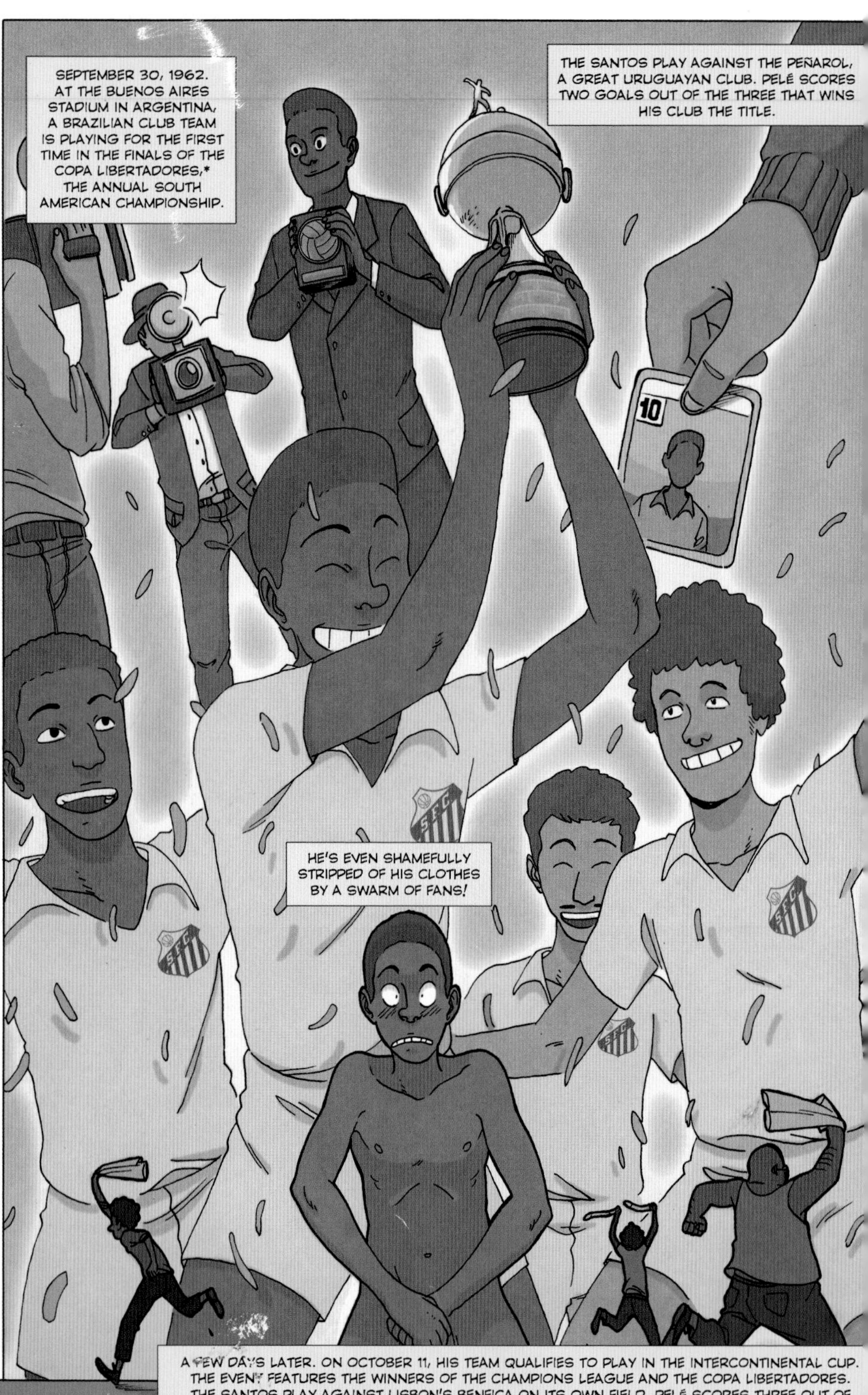
SEPTEMBER 30, 1962. AT THE BUENOS AIRES STADIUM IN ARGENTINA, A BRAZILIAN CLUB TEAM IS PLAYING FOR THE FIRST TIME IN THE FINALS OF THE COPA LIBERTADORES,* THE ANNUAL SOUTH AMERICAN CHAMPIONSHIP.
THE SANTOS PLAY AGAINST THE PEÑAROL, A GREAT URUGUAYAN CLUB. PELÉ SCORES TWO GOALS OUT OF THE THREE THAT WINS HIS CLUB THE TITLE.
10
HE'S EVEN SHAMEFULLY STRIPPED OF HIS CLOTHES BY A SWARM OF FANS!
A FEW DAYS LATER. ON OCTOBER 11, HIS TEAM QUALIFIES TO PLAY IN THE INTERCONTINENTAL CUP. THE EVENT FEATURES THE WINNERS OF THE CHAMPIONS LEAGUE AND THE COPA LIBERTADORES. THE SANTOS PLAY AGAINST LISBON'S BENFICA ON ITS OWN FIELD. PELÉ SCORES THREE OUT OF THE FIVE GOALS THAT BRING HIS TEAM THE FAMOUS TROPHY.

*THE LIBERATORS CU

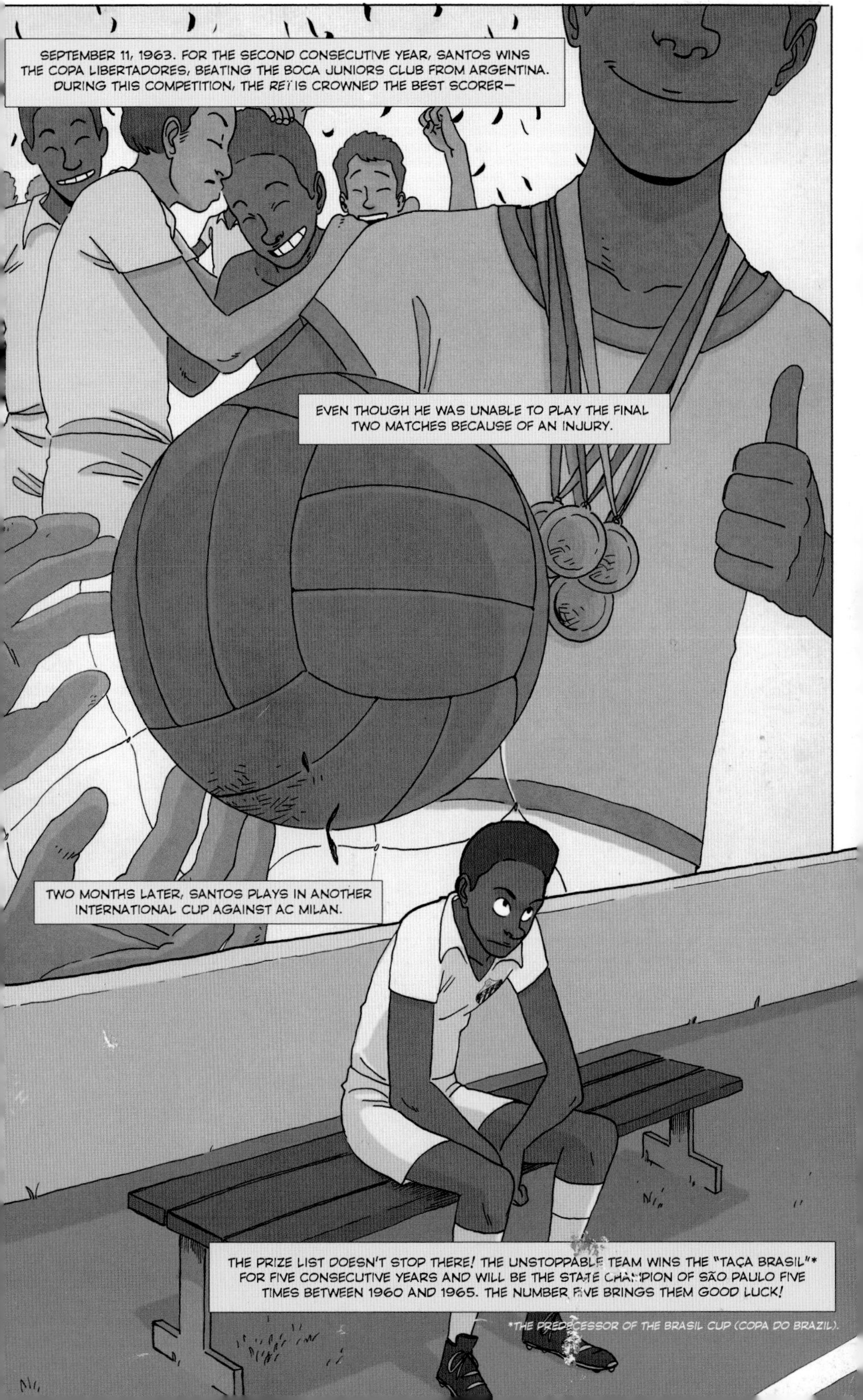
SEPTEMBER 11, 1963. FOR THE SECOND CONSECUTIVE YEAR, SANTOS WINS THE COPA LIBERTADORES, BEATING THE BOCA JUNIORS CLUB FROM ARGENTINA. DURING THIS COMPETITION, THE *REI* IS CROWNED THE BEST SCORER—
EVEN THOUGH HE WAS UNABLE TO PLAY THE FINAL TWO MATCHES BECAUSE OF AN INJURY.
TWO MONTHS LATER, SANTOS PLAYS IN ANOTHER INTERNATIONAL CUP AGAINST AC MILAN.
THE PRIZE LIST DOESN'T STOP THERE! THE UNSTOPPABLE TEAM WINS THE "TAÇA BRASIL"* FOR FIVE CONSECUTIVE YEARS AND WILL BE THE STATE CHAMPION OF SÃO PAULO FIVE TIMES BETWEEN 1960 AND 1965. THE NUMBER FIVE BRINGS THEM GOOD LUCK!
*THE PREDECESSOR OF THE BRASIL CUP (COPA DO BRAZIL).

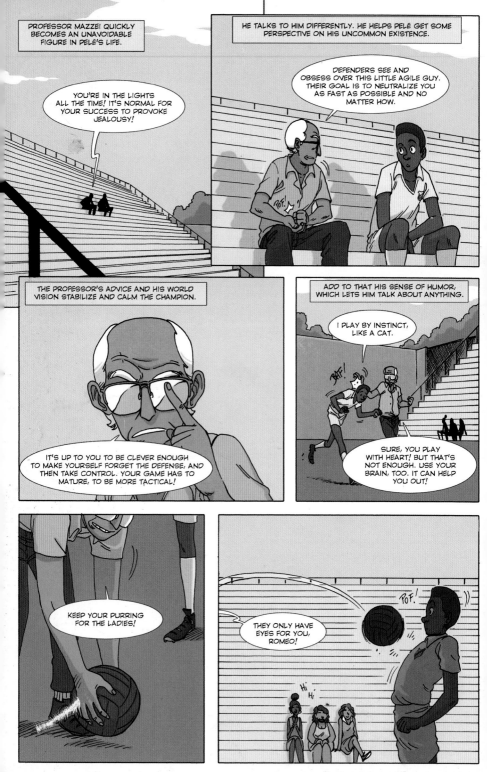

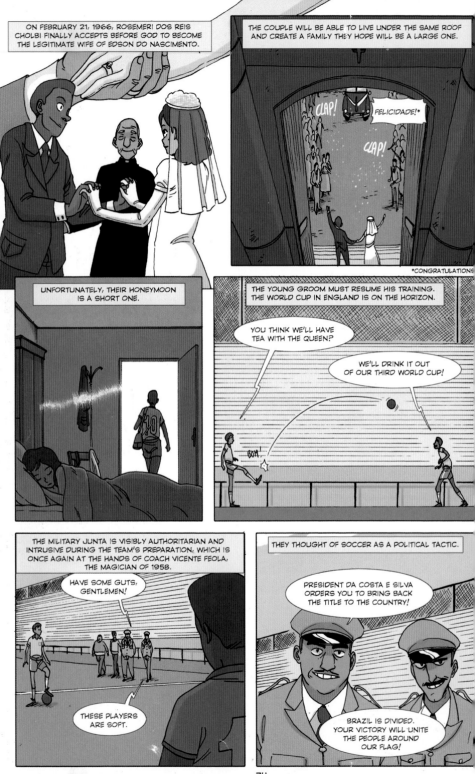

ON FEBRUARY 21, 1966, ROSEMERI DOS REIS CHOLBI FINALLY ACCEPTS BEFORE GOD TO BECOME THE LEGITIMATE WIFE OF EDSON DO NASCIMENTO.

THE COUPLE WILL BE ABLE TO LIVE UNDER THE SAME ROOF AND CREATE A FAMILY THEY HOPE WILL BE A LARGE ONE.

CLAP!

FELICIDADE!*

CLAP!

*CONGRATULATIONS

UNFORTUNATELY, THEIR HONEYMOON IS A SHORT ONE.

THE YOUNG GROOM MUST RESUME HIS TRAINING. THE WORLD CUP IN ENGLAND IS ON THE HORIZON.

YOU THINK WE'LL HAVE TEA WITH THE QUEEN?

WE'LL DRINK IT OUT OF OUR THIRD WORLD CUP!

BOM

THE MILITARY JUNTA IS VISIBLY AUTHORITARIAN AND INTRUSIVE DURING THE TEAM'S PREPARATION, WHICH IS ONCE AGAIN AT THE HANDS OF COACH VICENTE FEOLA, THE MAGICIAN OF 1958.

HAVE SOME GUTS, GENTLEMEN!

THESE PLAYERS ARE SOFT.

THEY THOUGHT OF SOCCER AS A POLITICAL TACTIC.

PRESIDENT DA COSTA E SILVA ORDERS YOU TO BRING BACK THE TITLE TO THE COUNTRY!

BRAZIL IS DIVIDED. YOUR VICTORY WILL UNITE THE PEOPLE AROUND OUR FLAG!

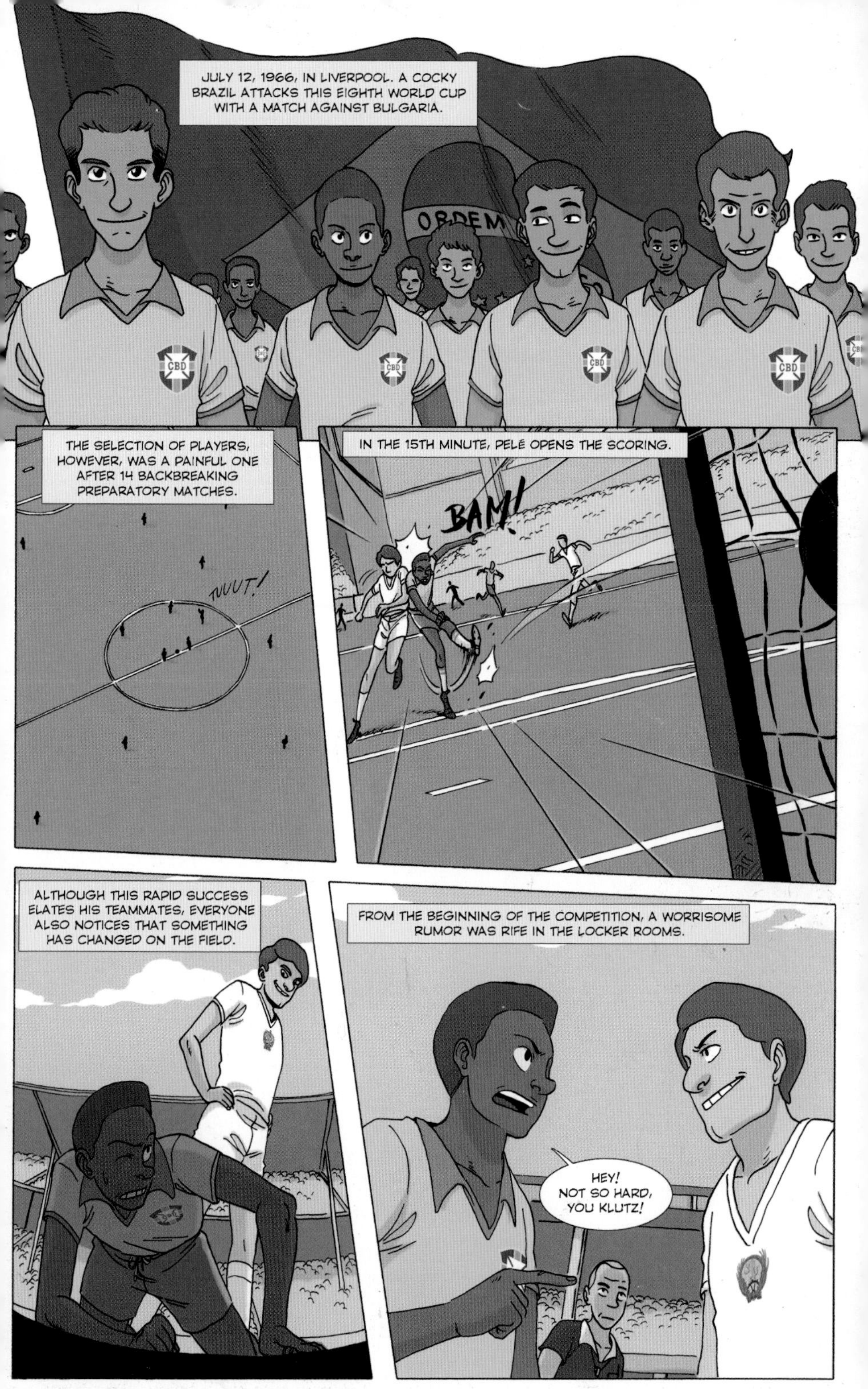
JULY 12, 1966, IN LIVERPOOL. A COCKY BRAZIL ATTACKS THIS EIGHTH WORLD CUP WITH A MATCH AGAINST BULGARIA.
ORDEM
CBD
THE SELECTION OF PLAYERS, HOWEVER, WAS A PAINFUL ONE AFTER 14 BACKBREAKING PREPARATORY MATCHES.
TUUUT!
IN THE 15TH MINUTE, PELÉ OPENS THE SCORING.
BAM!
ALTHOUGH THIS RAPID SUCCESS ELATES HIS TEAMMATES, EVERYONE ALSO NOTICES THAT SOMETHING HAS CHANGED ON THE FIELD.
FROM THE BEGINNING OF THE COMPETITION, A WORRISOME RUMOR WAS RIFE IN THE LOCKER ROOMS.
HEY! NOT SO HARD, YOU KLUTZ!

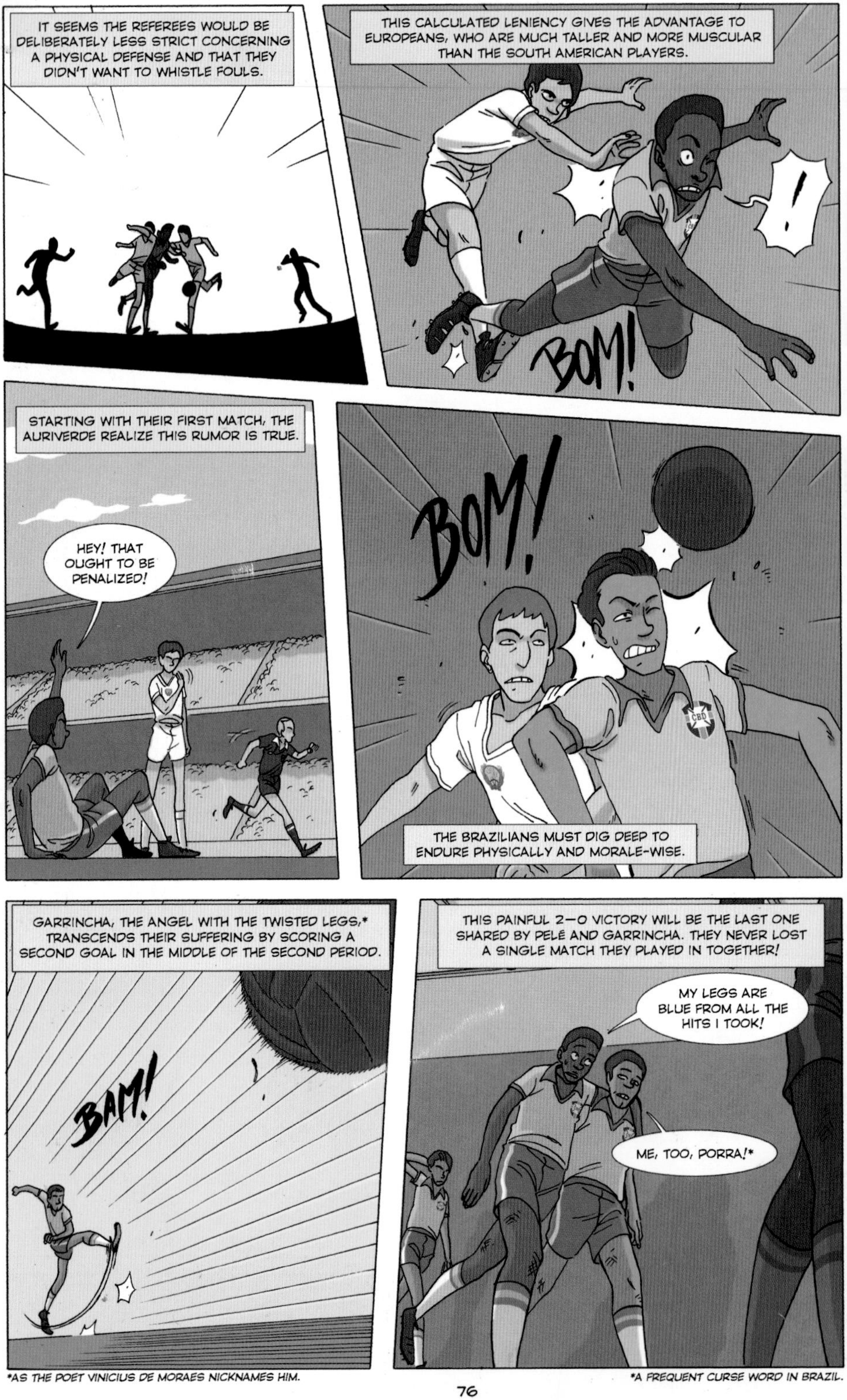
IT SEEMS THE REFEREES WOULD BE DELIBERATELY LESS STRICT CONCERNING A PHYSICAL DEFENSE AND THAT THEY DIDN'T WANT TO WHISTLE FOULS.
THIS CALCULATED LENIENCY GIVES THE ADVANTAGE TO EUROPEANS, WHO ARE MUCH TALLER AND MORE MUSCULAR THAN THE SOUTH AMERICAN PLAYERS.
!
BOM!
STARTING WITH THEIR FIRST MATCH, THE AURIVERDE REALIZE THIS RUMOR IS TRUE.
HEY! THAT OUGHT TO BE PENALIZED!
BOM!
THE BRAZILIANS MUST DIG DEEP TO ENDURE PHYSICALLY AND MORALE-WISE.
GARRINCHA, THE ANGEL WITH THE TWISTED LEGS,* TRANSCENDS THEIR SUFFERING BY SCORING A SECOND GOAL IN THE MIDDLE OF THE SECOND PERIOD.
BAM!
THIS PAINFUL 2–0 VICTORY WILL BE THE LAST ONE SHARED BY PELÉ AND GARRINCHA. THEY NEVER LOST A SINGLE MATCH THEY PLAYED IN TOGETHER!
MY LEGS ARE BLUE FROM ALL THE HITS I TOOK!
ME, TOO, PORRA!*

*AS THE POET VINICIUS DE MORAES NICKNAMES HIM.

*A FREQUENT CURSE WORD IN BRAZIL.

JULY 19, LIVERPOOL'S STADIUM. THE INEXPERIENCED PORTUGAL MAKES THEIR WORLD CUP DEBUT IN A MATCH AGAINST BRAZIL.

FROM THE BEGINNING OF THE MATCH, PELÉ IS ATTACKED ON ALL SIDES BY HIS OPPONENTS...

...WHO HAMMER AWAY AT HIS WOUNDED KNEE.

BAF!

BOM

THE PORTUGUESE DEFENDER JOÃO MORAIS MULTIPLIES THE BRUTAL TACKLES WITH NO INTERFERENCE FROM THE REFEREE.

"I STARTED THE JOB, MORAIS FINISHED IT," BULGARIAN DEFENDER ZHECHEV WILL ADMIT LATER. THE DESTRUCTIVE EFFORTS, IN FACT, END UP GETTING RID OF PELÉ!

SHBAH!

BRAF!

WHILE THE REY IS FALLING, THE SAME DEFENDER FLATTENS HIM VIOLENTLY, LEGS OUTSTRETCHED, AS IF TO BREAK HIM FOR GOOD.

YOU HAVE A TORN KNEE LIGAMENT!

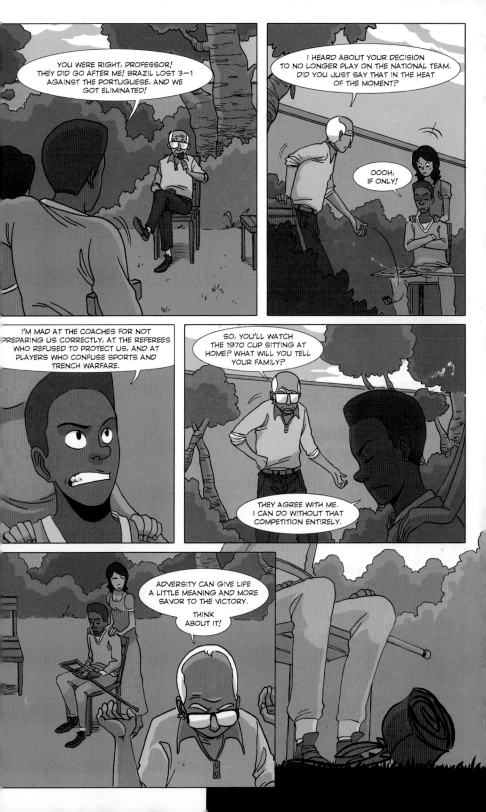

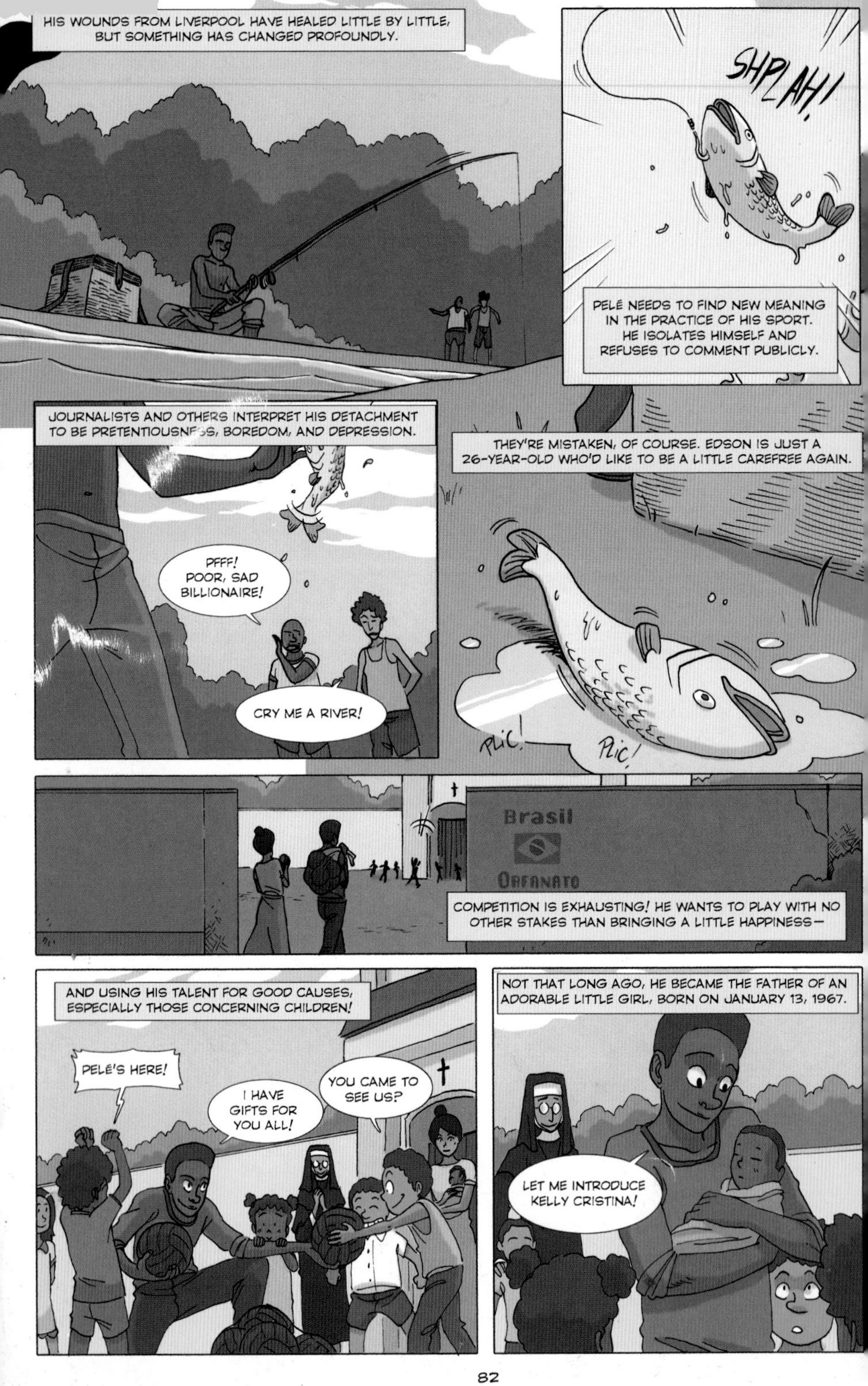

HIS WOUNDS FROM LIVERPOOL HAVE HEALED LITTLE BY LITTLE, BUT SOMETHING HAS CHANGED PROFOUNDLY.
SHPLAH!
PELÉ NEEDS TO FIND NEW MEANING IN THE PRACTICE OF HIS SPORT. HE ISOLATES HIMSELF AND REFUSES TO COMMENT PUBLICLY.
JOURNALISTS AND OTHERS INTERPRET HIS DETACHMENT TO BE PRETENTIOUSNESS, BOREDOM, AND DEPRESSION.
PFFF! POOR, SAD BILLIONAIRE!
CRY ME A RIVER!
THEY'RE MISTAKEN, OF COURSE. EDSON IS JUST A 26-YEAR-OLD WHO'D LIKE TO BE A LITTLE CAREFREE AGAIN.
PLIC!
PLIC!
Brasil
ORFANATO
COMPETITION IS EXHAUSTING! HE WANTS TO PLAY WITH NO OTHER STAKES THAN BRINGING A LITTLE HAPPINESS—
AND USING HIS TALENT FOR GOOD CAUSES, ESPECIALLY THOSE CONCERNING CHILDREN!
PELÉ'S HERE!
I HAVE GIFTS FOR YOU ALL!
YOU CAME TO SEE US?
NOT THAT LONG AGO, HE BECAME THE FATHER OF AN ADORABLE LITTLE GIRL, BORN ON JANUARY 13, 1967.
LET ME INTRODUCE KELLY CRISTINA!

Halftime!
The 1,000th

"Scoring one thousand goals like Pelé isn't the most difficult or most extraordinary thing. Scoring one goal like Pelé is."
—Carlos Drummond de Andrade, Brazilian poet

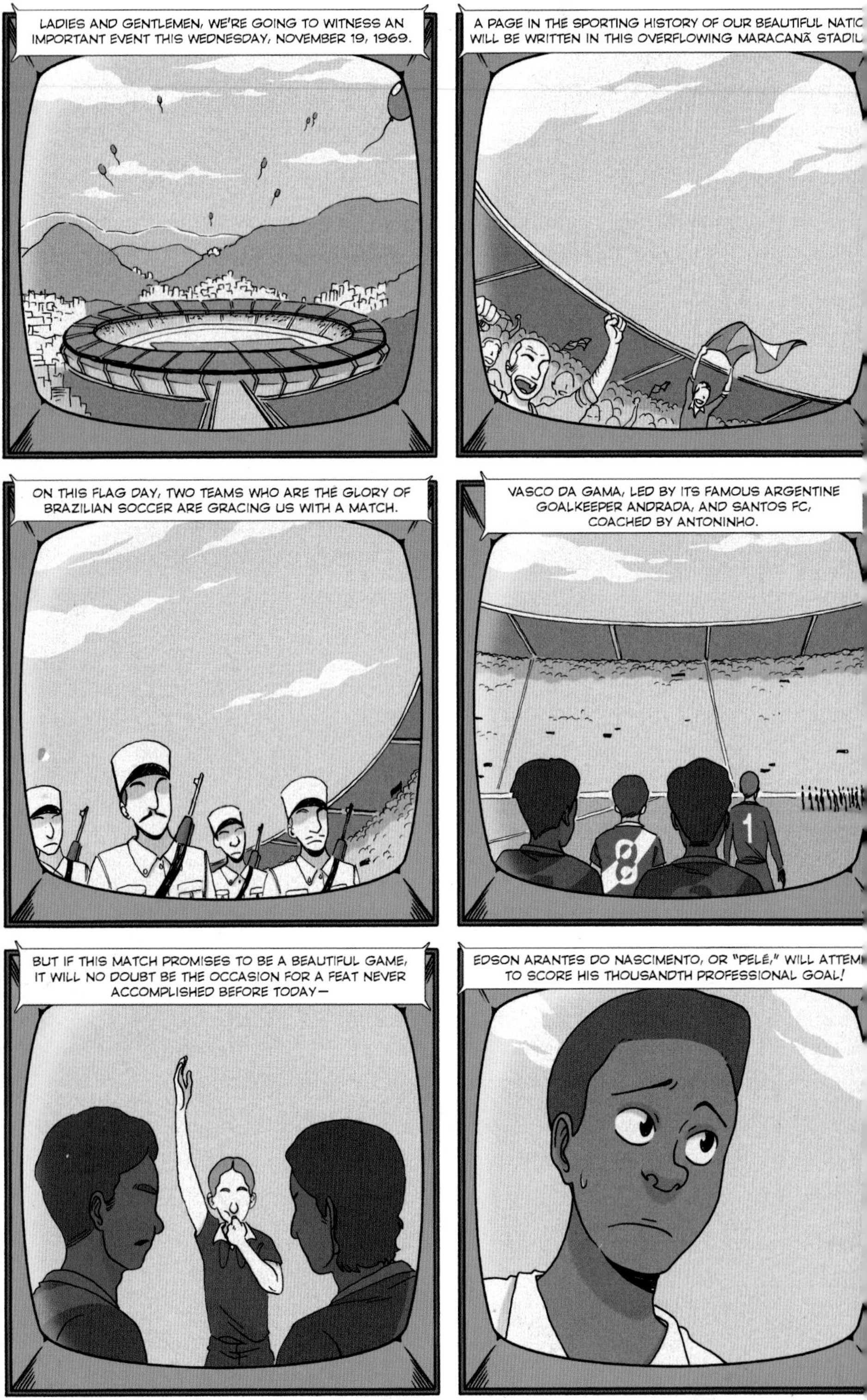
LADIES AND GENTLEMEN, WE'RE GOING TO WITNESS AN IMPORTANT EVENT THIS WEDNESDAY, NOVEMBER 19, 1969.
A PAGE IN THE SPORTING HISTORY OF OUR BEAUTIFUL NATIO
WILL BE WRITTEN IN THIS OVERFLOWING MARACANÃ STADIU
ON THIS FLAG DAY, TWO TEAMS WHO ARE THE GLORY OF BRAZILIAN SOCCER ARE GRACING US WITH A MATCH.
VASCO DA GAMA, LED BY ITS FAMOUS ARGENTINE GOALKEEPER ANDRADA, AND SANTOS FC, COACHED BY ANTONINHO.
BUT IF THIS MATCH PROMISES TO BE A BEAUTIFUL GAME, IT WILL NO DOUBT BE THE OCCASION FOR A FEAT NEVER ACCOMPLISHED BEFORE TODAY—
EDSON ARANTES DO NASCIMENTO, OR "PELÉ," WILL ATTEM
TO SCORE HIS THOUSANDTH PROFESSIONAL GOAL!

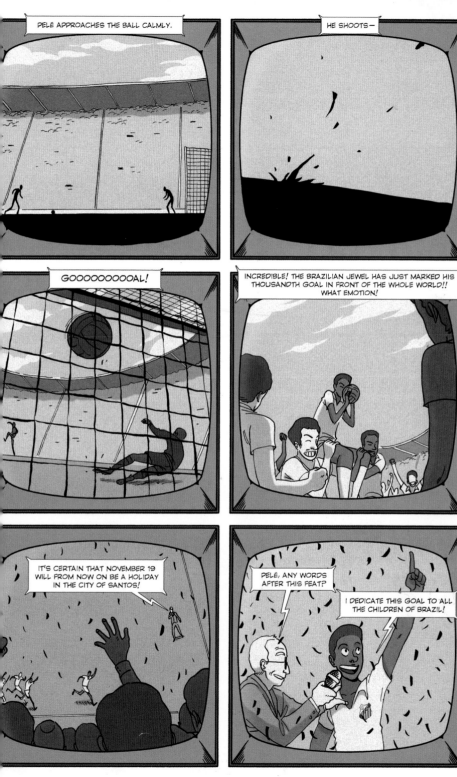

89

Chapter 6
Never Two Without Three!

"Before the match, I told myself: he's just flesh and bones, like me.
Later I understood I was mistaken."
—Tarcisio Burgnich, defender for the Italian national team

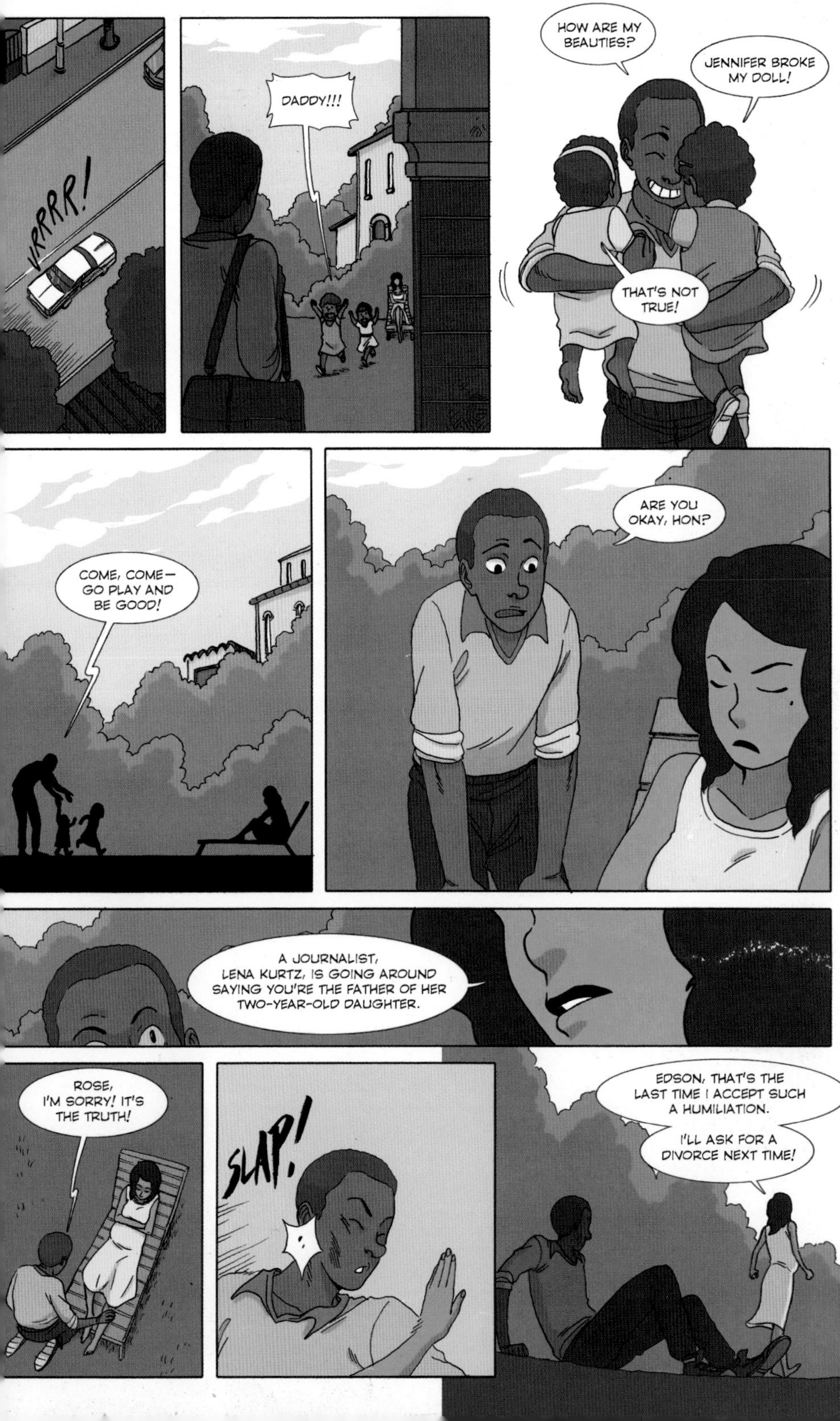
VRRRR!
DADDY!!!
HOW ARE MY BEAUTIES?
JENNIFER BROKE MY DOLL!
THAT'S NOT TRUE!
COME, COME— GO PLAY AND BE GOOD!
ARE YOU OKAY, HON?
A JOURNALIST, LENA KURTZ, IS GOING AROUND SAYING YOU'RE THE FATHER OF HER TWO-YEAR-OLD DAUGHTER.
ROSE, I'M SORRY! IT'S THE TRUTH!
SLAP!
EDSON, THAT'S THE LAST TIME I ACCEPT SUCH A HUMILIATION.
I'LL ASK FOR A DIVORCE NEXT TIME!

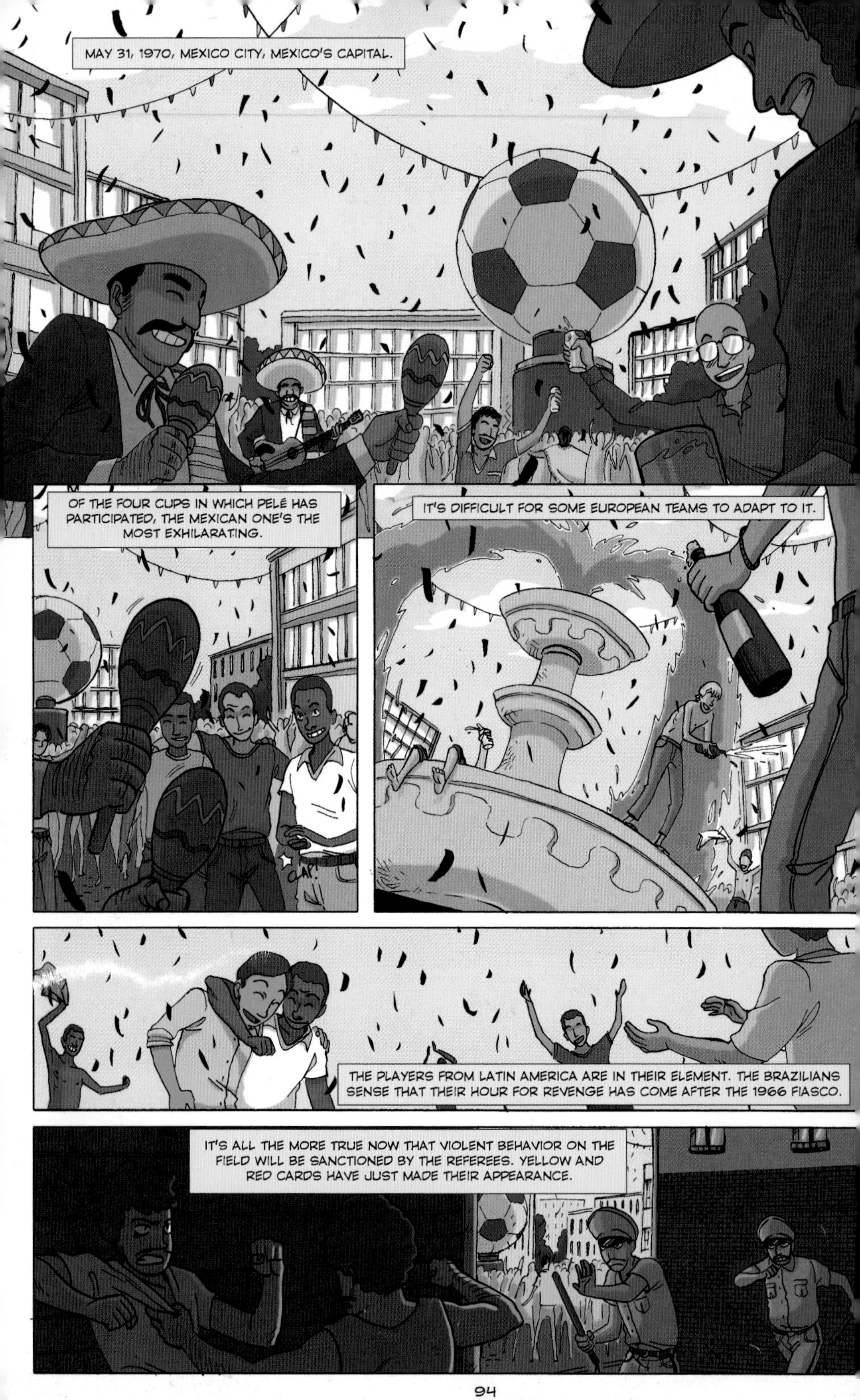

MAY 31, 1970, MEXICO CITY, MEXICO'S CAPITAL.
OF THE FOUR CUPS IN WHICH PELÉ HAS PARTICIPATED, THE MEXICAN ONE'S THE MOST EXHILARATING.
CLAP!
IT'S DIFFICULT FOR SOME EUROPEAN TEAMS TO ADAPT TO IT.
THE PLAYERS FROM LATIN AMERICA ARE IN THEIR ELEMENT. THE BRAZILIANS SENSE THAT THEIR HOUR FOR REVENGE HAS COME AFTER THE 1966 FIASCO.
IT'S ALL THE MORE TRUE NOW THAT VIOLENT BEHAVIOR ON THE FIELD WILL BE SANCTIONED BY THE REFEREES. YELLOW AND RED CARDS HAVE JUST MADE THEIR APPEARANCE.

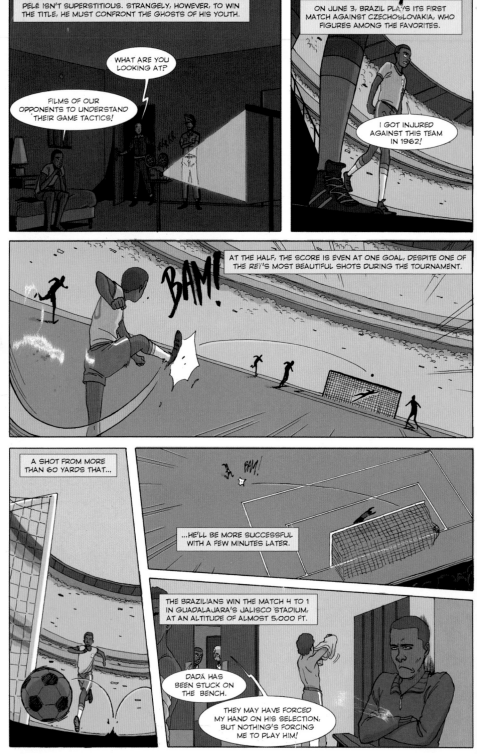

THE NEXT DAY, DURING THE PREPARATION FOR THE SECOND MATCH OF THE FIRST ROUND, AGAINST ENGLAND—

THE NEWSPAPER HEADLINE IS "THE CLASH OF THE CHAMPIONS"!

A SETTLING OF SCORES BETWEEN THE LAST TWO WINNERS OF THE CUP!

THIS IS NO DOUBT THE MOST ANTICIPATED MATCH IN THE HISTORY OF SOCCER!

FOR ALL THAT, IT WON'T BE A SIMPLE SAMBA PARADE!

TOO BAD—

AND DON'T BET ON SCORING QUICKLY AND EASILY!

GORDON BANKS IS AN EXCELLENT GOALIE WHO WON'T LET ANYTHING ENTER HIS NETS.

BAM!

A SINGLE GOAL WILL BE ENOUGH TO SHOW WE'RE WAY BETTER THAN THOSE BLOODY BRITS!

BAM!

FINAL SCORE: BRAZIL 1 — ENGLAND 0.

CLAP!

SNIFF! IT'S THE MOST BEAUTIFUL MATCH I'VE EVER SEEN!

97

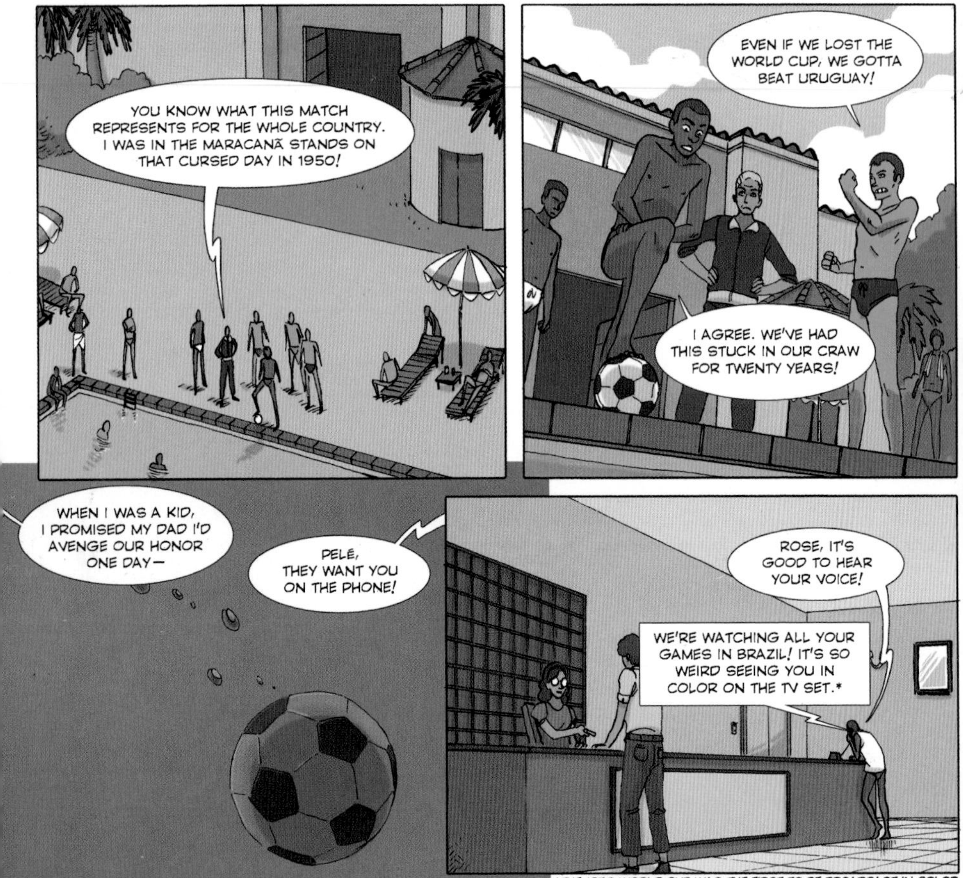

YOU KNOW WHAT THIS MATCH REPRESENTS FOR THE WHOLE COUNTRY. I WAS IN THE MARACANÃ STANDS ON THAT CURSED DAY IN 1950!
EVEN IF WE LOST THE WORLD CUP, WE GOTTA BEAT URUGUAY!
I AGREE. WE'VE HAD THIS STUCK IN OUR CRAW FOR TWENTY YEARS!
WHEN I WAS A KID, I PROMISED MY DAD I'D AVENGE OUR HONOR ONE DAY—
PELÉ, THEY WANT YOU ON THE PHONE!
ROSE, IT'S GOOD TO HEAR YOUR VOICE!
WE'RE WATCHING ALL YOUR GAMES IN BRAZIL! IT'S SO WEIRD SEEING YOU IN COLOR ON THE TV SET.*

*THE 1970 WORLD CUP WAS THE FIRST TO BE BROADCAST IN COLOR.

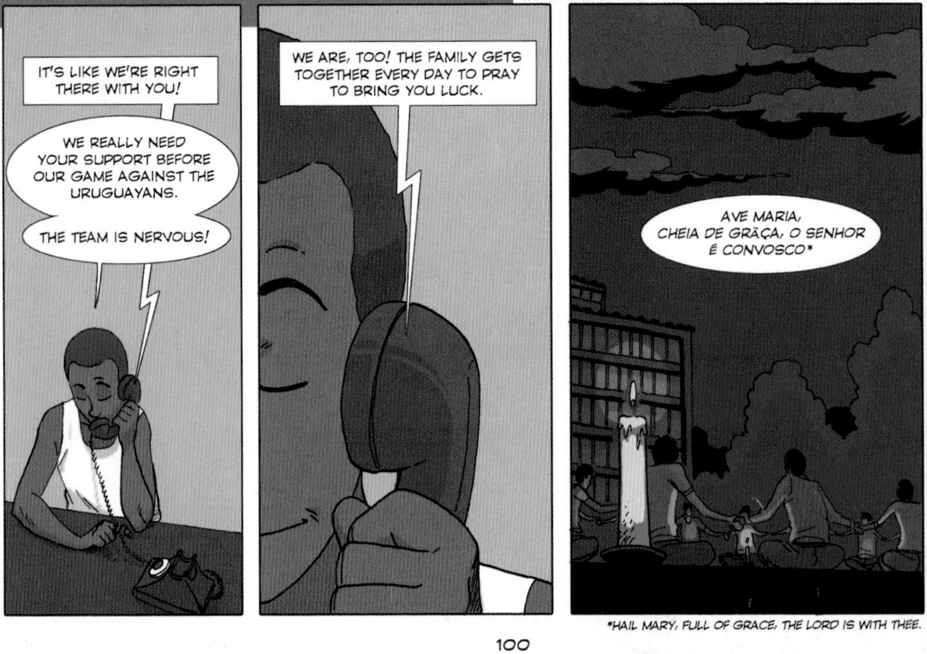

IT'S LIKE WE'RE RIGHT THERE WITH YOU!
WE REALLY NEED YOUR SUPPORT BEFORE OUR GAME AGAINST THE URUGUAYANS.
THE TEAM IS NERVOUS!
WE ARE, TOO! THE FAMILY GETS TOGETHER EVERY DAY TO PRAY TO BRING YOU LUCK.
AVE MARIA, CHEIA DE GRAÇA, O SENHOR É CONVOSCO*

*HAIL MARY, FULL OF GRACE, THE LORD IS WITH THEE.

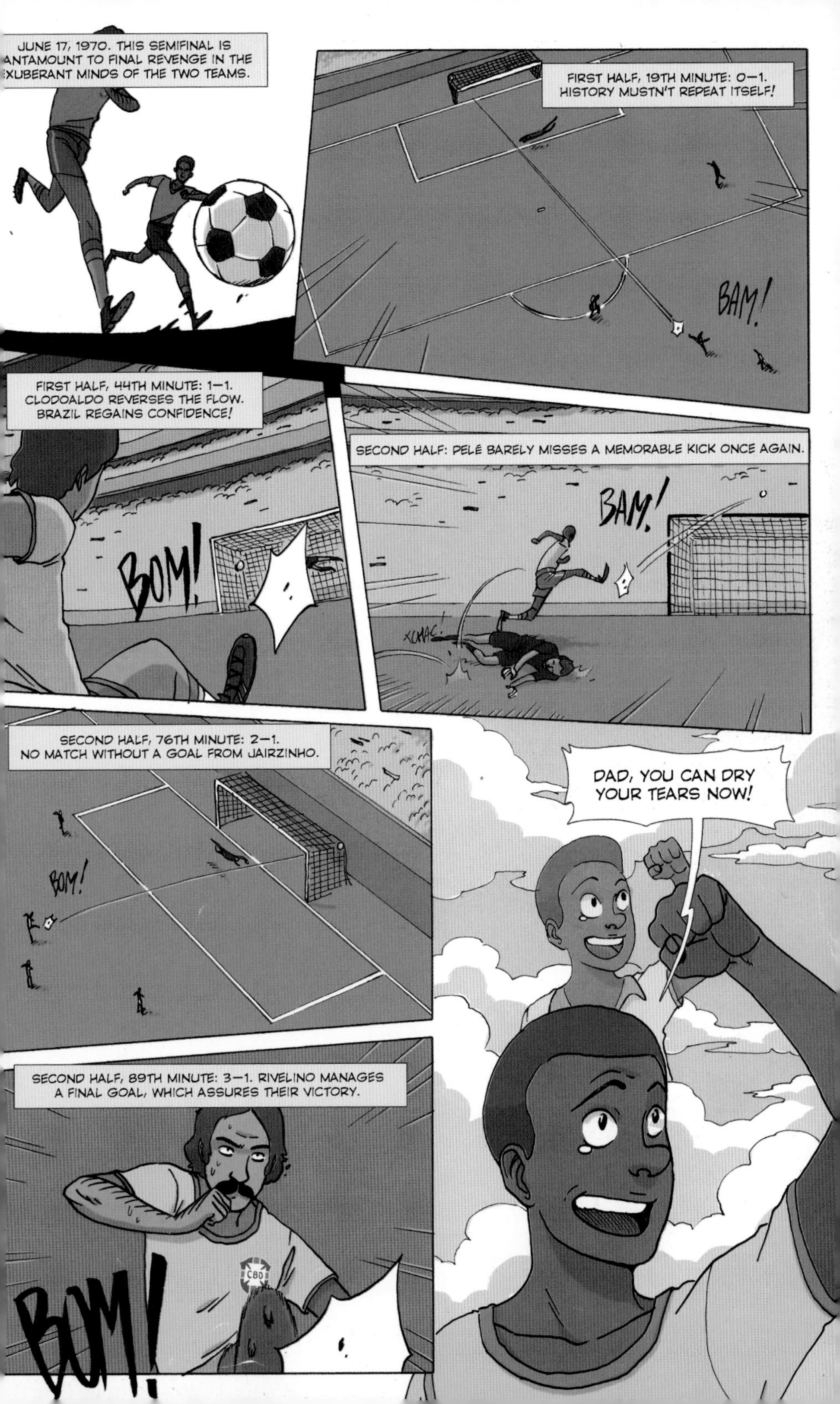
JUNE 17, 1970. THIS SEMIFINAL IS TANTAMOUNT TO FINAL REVENGE IN THE EXUBERANT MINDS OF THE TWO TEAMS.
FIRST HALF, 19TH MINUTE: 0–1. HISTORY MUSTN'T REPEAT ITSELF!
BAM!
FIRST HALF, 44TH MINUTE: 1–1. CLODOALDO REVERSES THE FLOW. BRAZIL REGAINS CONFIDENCE!
BOM!
SECOND HALF: PELÉ BARELY MISSES A MEMORABLE KICK ONCE AGAIN.
BAM!
SECOND HALF, 76TH MINUTE: 2–1. NO MATCH WITHOUT A GOAL FROM JAIRZINHO.
BOM!
DAD, YOU CAN DRY YOUR TEARS NOW!
SECOND HALF, 89TH MINUTE: 3–1. RIVELINO MANAGES A FINAL GOAL, WHICH ASSURES THEIR VICTORY.
CBD
BOM!

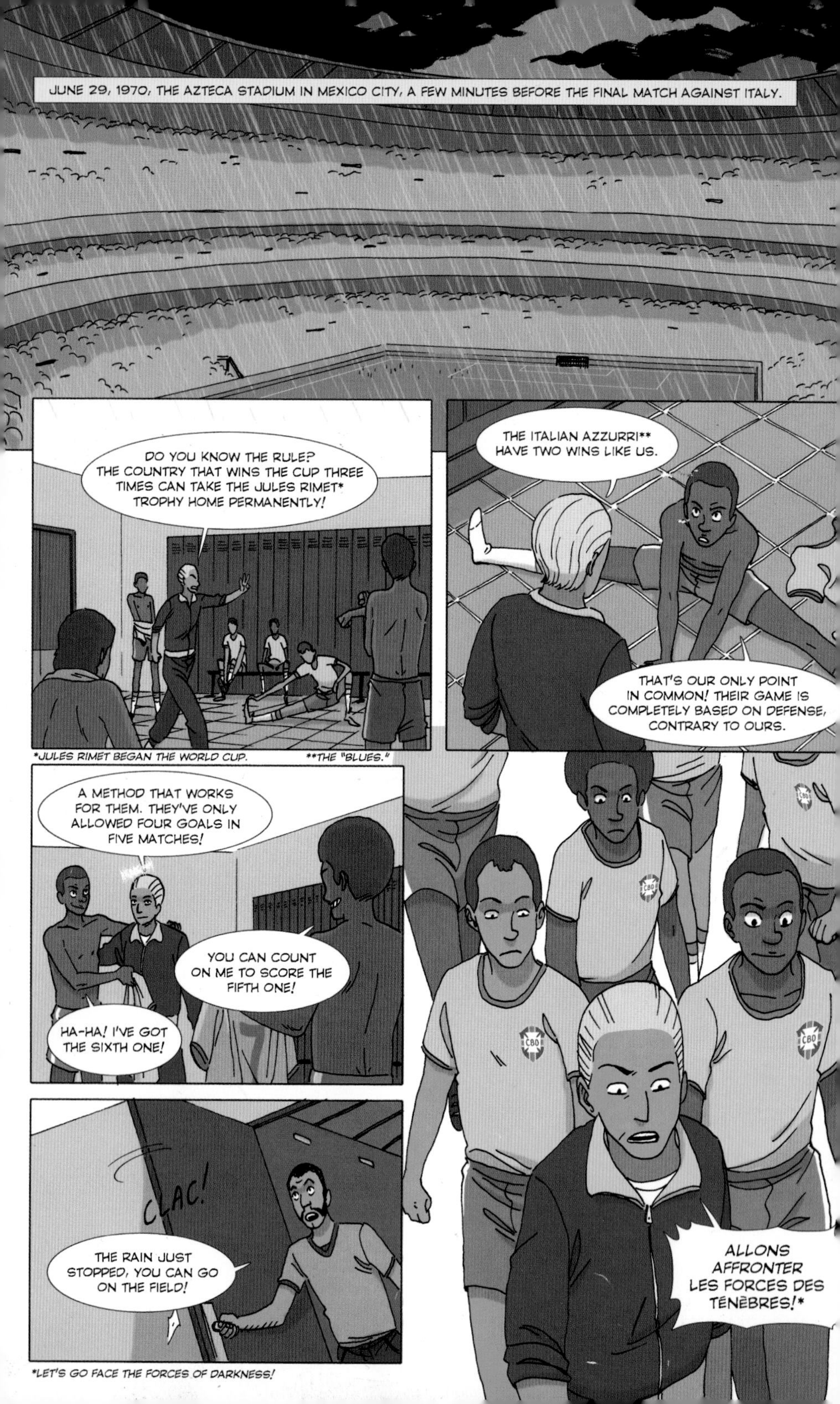

JUNE 29, 1970, THE AZTECA STADIUM IN MEXICO CITY, A FEW MINUTES BEFORE THE FINAL MATCH AGAINST ITALY.
DO YOU KNOW THE RULE? THE COUNTRY THAT WINS THE CUP THREE TIMES CAN TAKE THE JULES RIMET* TROPHY HOME PERMANENTLY!
THE ITALIAN AZZURRI** HAVE TWO WINS LIKE US.
THAT'S OUR ONLY POINT IN COMMON! THEIR GAME IS COMPLETELY BASED ON DEFENSE, CONTRARY TO OURS.
*JULES RIMET BEGAN THE WORLD CUP.
**THE "BLUES."
A METHOD THAT WORKS FOR THEM. THEY'VE ONLY ALLOWED FOUR GOALS IN FIVE MATCHES!
YOU CAN COUNT ON ME TO SCORE THE FIFTH ONE!
HA-HA! I'VE GOT THE SIXTH ONE!
CLAC!
THE RAIN JUST STOPPED, YOU CAN GO ON THE FIELD!
ALLONS AFFRONTER LES FORCES DES TÉNÈBRES!*
*LET'S GO FACE THE FORCES OF DARKNESS!

THE YEAR AFTER HIS SUCCESS ON MEXICAN GROUNDS, PELÉ IS GIVING A SPEECH—

THIS FRIENDLY MATCH AGAINST YUGOSLAVIA WILL BE MY LAST ONE IN THE *SELEÇÃO!*

ON JULY 18, 1971, IN AN OVERFLOWING MARACANÃ STADIUM, HE BIDS HIS FINAL FAREWELL TO INTERNATIONAL COMPETITION.

FICA! FICA!*

FLASH!

*STAY!

THIS DECISION ISN'T TO EVERYBODY'S LIKING, SOME OF WHOM RESORT TO ALL (SOMETIMES HAREBRAINED) KINDS OF PRESSURE.

PELÉ IS UNDER THE JURISDICTION OF THE NATIONAL CONFEDERATION OF SPORTS. WE CAN FORCE HIM TO PLAY FOR BRAZIL!

?!

WHEREAS OTHERS ARE MORE TOUCHING, LIKE THE LETTER FROM A NEW PRESIDENT.

I HOPE TO RECEIVE THAT WORD OF ENCOURAGEMENT FOR THIS SPORT FOR WHICH YOU HAVE BECOME AN IDOL.

JOÃO HAVELANGE
PRESIDENT OF FIFA

FIFA

EVEN THE MILITARY WEIGH IN PUBLICLY IN AN ATTEMPT TO INFLUENCE HIM.

IT'D BE VERY IMPORTANT FOR HIM TO COME BACK! IT WOULD BE GOOD FOR THE COUNTRY!

BUT THIS TIME, NOTHING AND NOBODY WILL CHANGE HIS MIND.

MY MIND'S MADE UP! WHAT DO YOU THINK ABOUT IT?

AT 31, IT'S TIME TO SPARE YOUR BODY. YOU'VE ALREADY SACRIFICED A KIDNEY!*

I HOPE YOU WON'T REGRET IT!

WHEN YOU'RE NOT HERE, THE KIDS AND I ARE CAGED UP!

CONTRACTUALLY, HE STILL HAS TWO YEARS LEFT TO PLAY FOR SANTOS, THEN HE CAN THINK OF A COMPLETE RETIREMENT.

DESPEDIDA, FUTBOL!*

!

BOM!

*FOLLOWING A RIB BROKEN DURING A MATCH, PELÉ UNDERWENT THE REMOVAL OF HIS RIGHT KIDNEY.

*FAREWELL, SOCCER!

Chapter 7
The American Dream

"We had superstars in the United States, but nothing at the level of Pelé. Everyone wanted to touch him, shake his hand, get a photo with him."
—John O'Reilly, spokesperson for the New York Cosmos

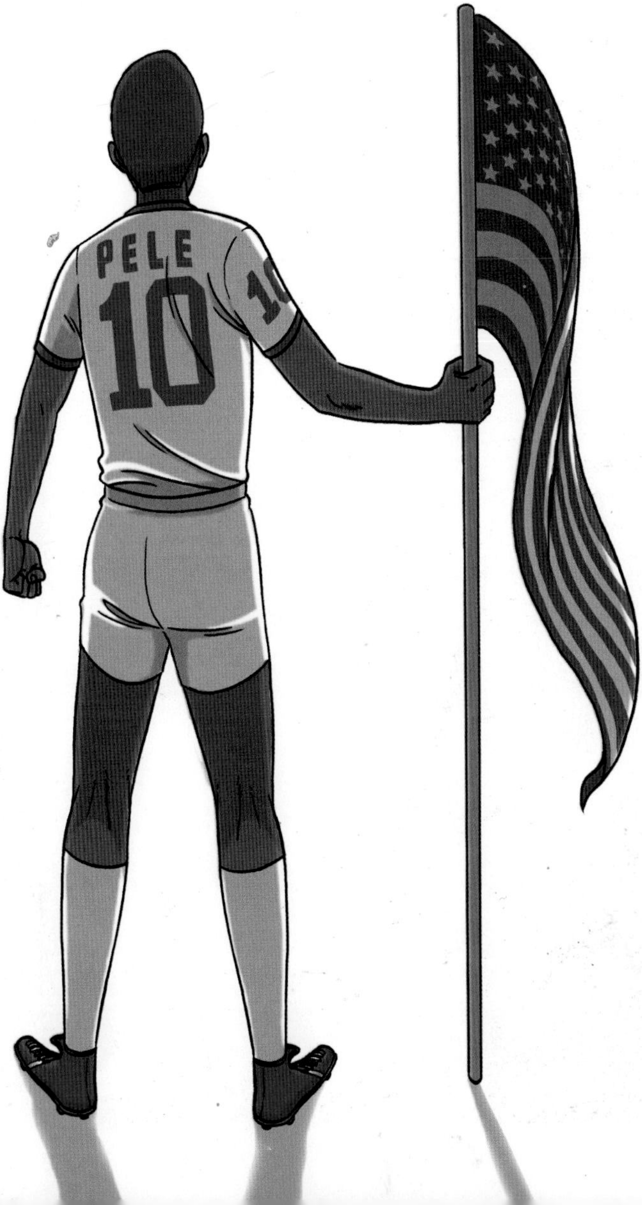

PELE
10

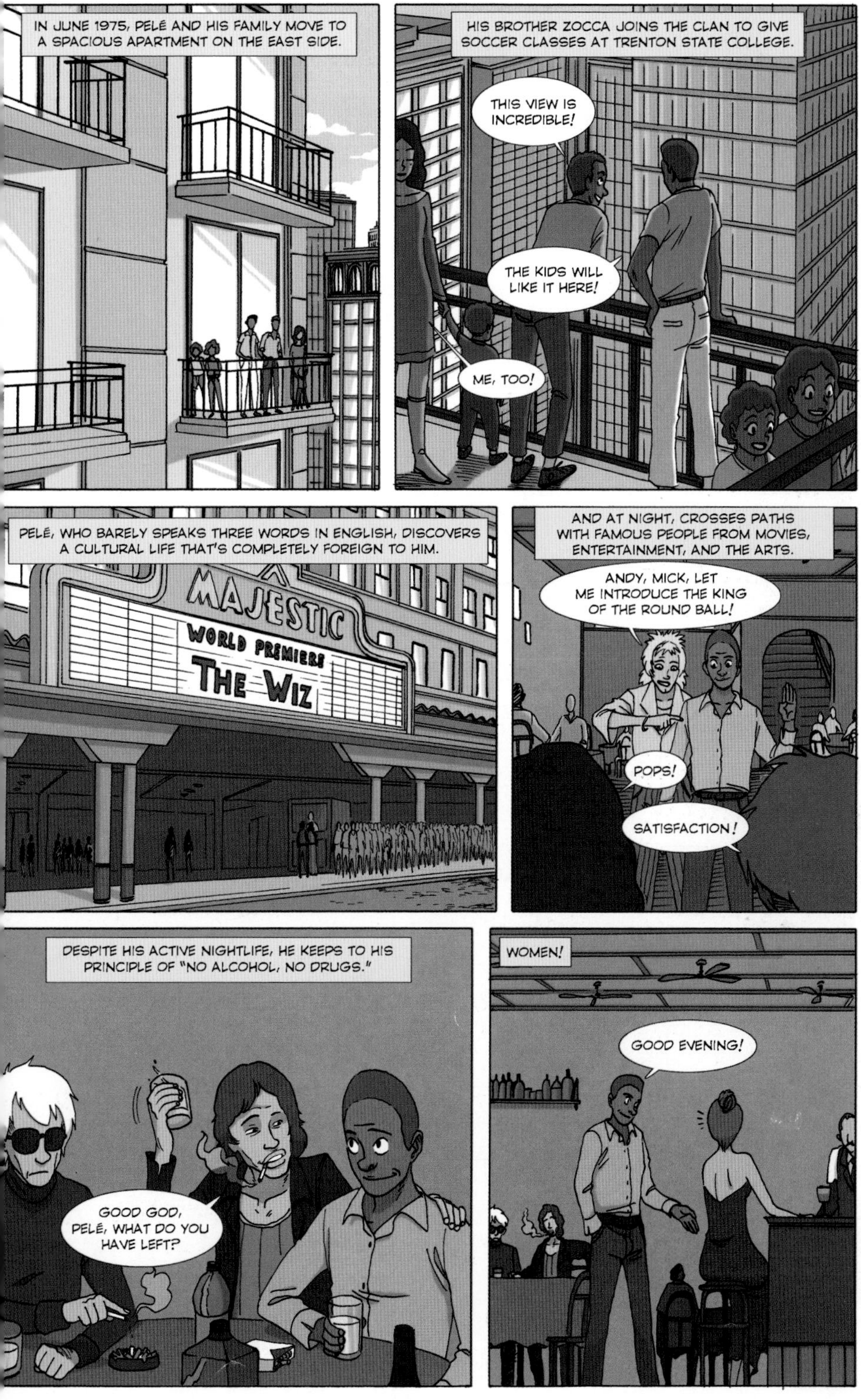

IN JUNE 1975, PELÉ AND HIS FAMILY MOVE TO A SPACIOUS APARTMENT ON THE EAST SIDE.
HIS BROTHER ZOCCA JOINS THE CLAN TO GIVE SOCCER CLASSES AT TRENTON STATE COLLEGE.
THIS VIEW IS INCREDIBLE!
THE KIDS WILL LIKE IT HERE!
ME, TOO!
PELÉ, WHO BARELY SPEAKS THREE WORDS IN ENGLISH, DISCOVERS A CULTURAL LIFE THAT'S COMPLETELY FOREIGN TO HIM.
MAJESTIC
WORLD PREMIERE
THE WIZ
AND AT NIGHT, CROSSES PATHS WITH FAMOUS PEOPLE FROM MOVIES, ENTERTAINMENT, AND THE ARTS.
ANDY, MICK, LET ME INTRODUCE THE KING OF THE ROUND BALL!
POPS!
SATISFACTION!
DESPITE HIS ACTIVE NIGHTLIFE, HE KEEPS TO HIS PRINCIPLE OF "NO ALCOHOL, NO DRUGS."
GOOD GOD, PELÉ, WHAT DO YOU HAVE LEFT?
WOMEN!
GOOD EVENING!

HOFSTRA UNIVERSITY'S STADIUM IN LONG ISLAND.

THE COSMOS'S GOAL IS TO QUALIFY FOR NASL'S* NORTH AMERICAN CHAMPIONSHIP.

ZUIP!

*NORTH AMERICAN SOCCER LEAGUE

ONLY, THE ARRIVAL OF THE NEW STAR IN MIDSEASON—

—COMBINED WITH HIS TEAMMATES' LACK OF TALENT, MAKES PROGRESS IMPOSSIBLE.

PLAY, FOR GOD'S SAKE! STOP WATCHING PELÉ!

WE HAVE TO WORK TOGETHER!

OKAY, COACH BRADLEY!

OKAY, MR. PELÉ!

MASNIK 3

CORREA 7

VLAMAS 5

FINI 12

WE DON'T STAND A CHANCE!

PELE 10

BOM!

FSH!

THIS IS ALL RIDICULOUS!

WHAT?! WHAT HAPPENED?

3

10

112

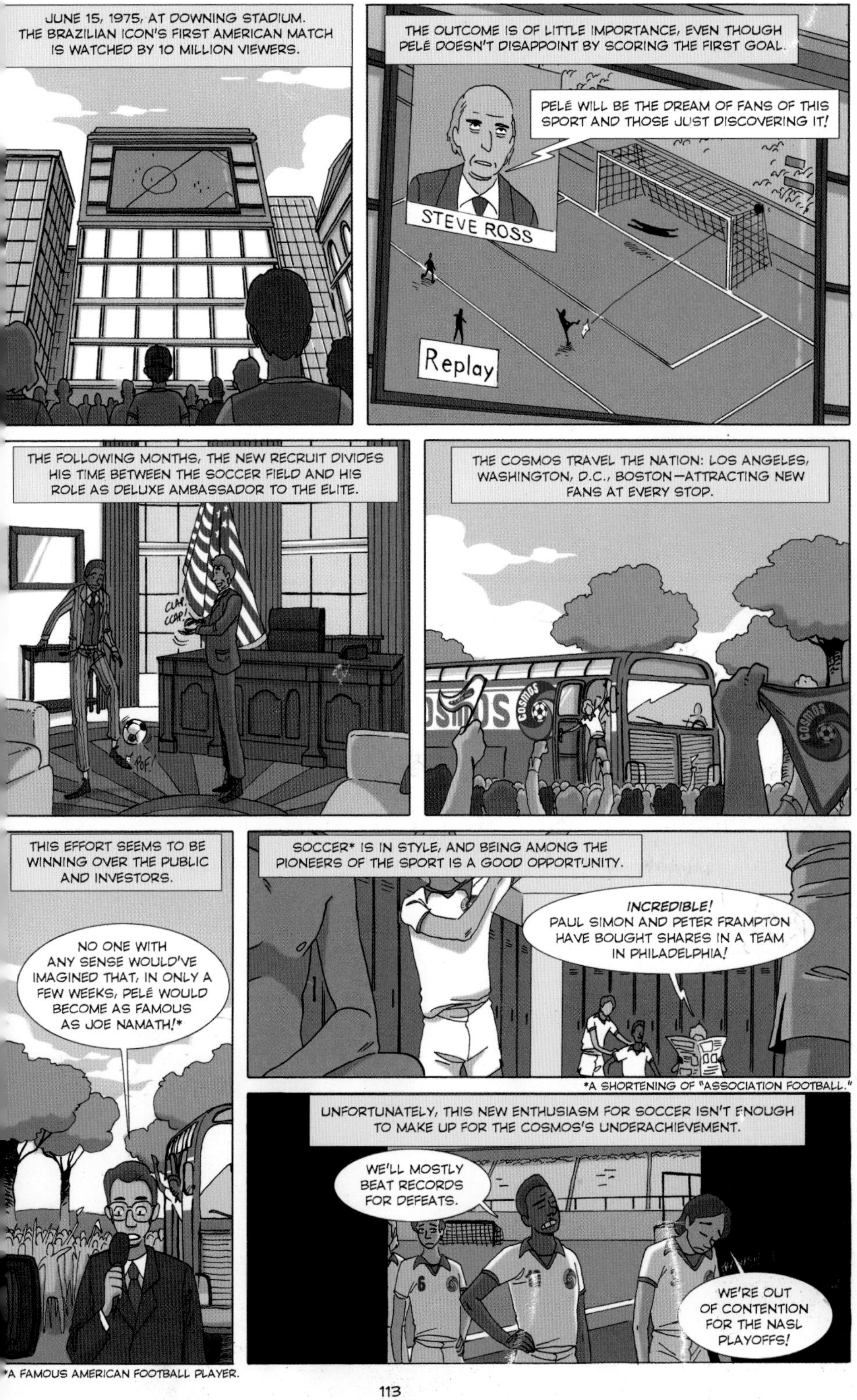
JUNE 15, 1975, AT DOWNING STADIUM. THE BRAZILIAN ICON'S FIRST AMERICAN MATCH IS WATCHED BY 10 MILLION VIEWERS.
THE OUTCOME IS OF LITTLE IMPORTANCE, EVEN THOUGH PELÉ DOESN'T DISAPPOINT BY SCORING THE FIRST GOAL.
PELÉ WILL BE THE DREAM OF FANS OF THIS SPORT AND THOSE JUST DISCOVERING IT!
STEVE ROSS
Replay
THE FOLLOWING MONTHS, THE NEW RECRUIT DIVIDES HIS TIME BETWEEN THE SOCCER FIELD AND HIS ROLE AS DELUXE AMBASSADOR TO THE ELITE.
CLAP! CLAP!
POF!
THE COSMOS TRAVEL THE NATION: LOS ANGELES, WASHINGTON, D.C., BOSTON—ATTRACTING NEW FANS AT EVERY STOP.
COSMOS
COSMOS
COSMOS
THIS EFFORT SEEMS TO BE WINNING OVER THE PUBLIC AND INVESTORS.
NO ONE WITH ANY SENSE WOULD'VE IMAGINED THAT, IN ONLY A FEW WEEKS, PELÉ WOULD BECOME AS FAMOUS AS JOE NAMATH!*
*A FAMOUS AMERICAN FOOTBALL PLAYER.
SOCCER* IS IN STYLE, AND BEING AMONG THE PIONEERS OF THE SPORT IS A GOOD OPPORTUNITY.
INCREDIBLE! PAUL SIMON AND PETER FRAMPTON HAVE BOUGHT SHARES IN A TEAM IN PHILADELPHIA!
*A SHORTENING OF "ASSOCIATION FOOTBALL."
UNFORTUNATELY, THIS NEW ENTHUSIASM FOR SOCCER ISN'T ENOUGH TO MAKE UP FOR THE COSMOS'S UNDERACHIEVEMENT.
WE'LL MOSTLY BEAT RECORDS FOR DEFEATS.
WE'RE OUT OF CONTENTION FOR THE NASL PLAYOFFS!

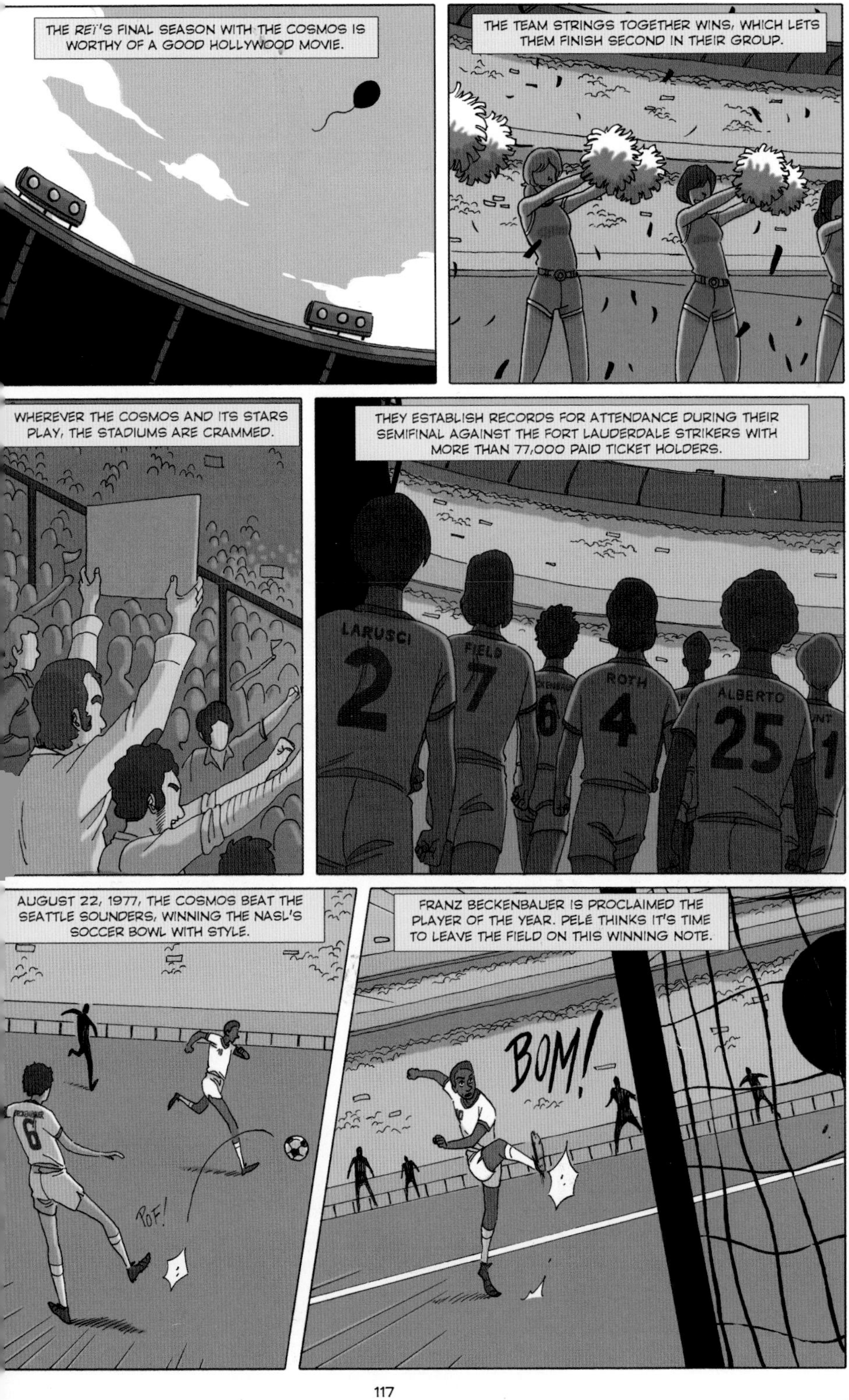
THE REI'S FINAL SEASON WITH THE COSMOS IS WORTHY OF A GOOD HOLLYWOOD MOVIE.
THE TEAM STRINGS TOGETHER WINS, WHICH LETS THEM FINISH SECOND IN THEIR GROUP.
WHEREVER THE COSMOS AND ITS STARS PLAY, THE STADIUMS ARE CRAMMED.
THEY ESTABLISH RECORDS FOR ATTENDANCE DURING THEIR SEMIFINAL AGAINST THE FORT LAUDERDALE STRIKERS WITH MORE THAN 77,000 PAID TICKET HOLDERS.
LARUSCI 2
FIELD 7
6
ROTH 4
ALBERTO 25
AUGUST 22, 1977, THE COSMOS BEAT THE SEATTLE SOUNDERS, WINNING THE NASL'S SOCCER BOWL WITH STYLE.
6
POF!
FRANZ BECKENBAUER IS PROCLAIMED THE PLAYER OF THE YEAR. PELÉ THINKS IT'S TIME TO LEAVE THE FIELD ON THIS WINNING NOTE.
BOM!

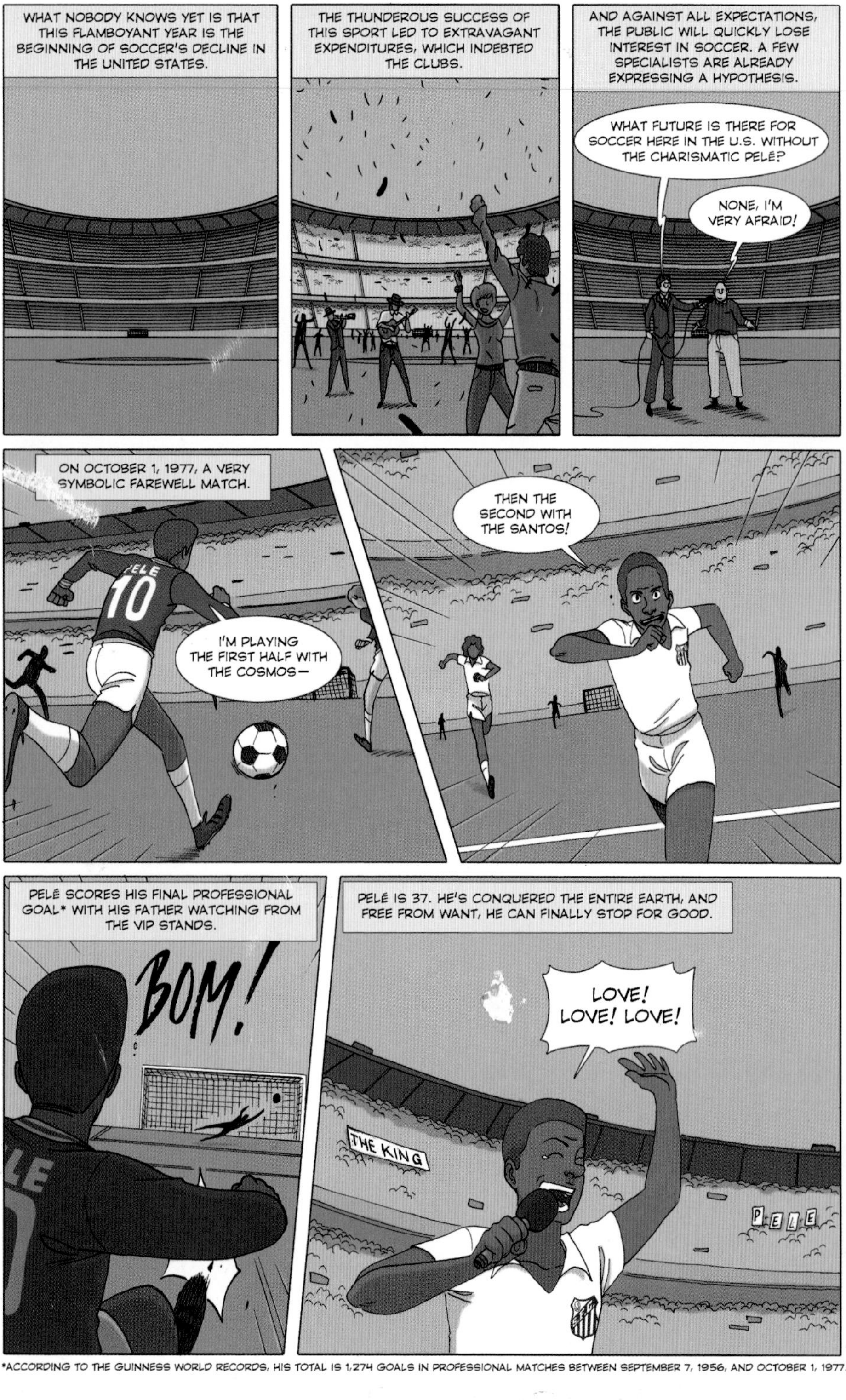
WHAT NOBODY KNOWS YET IS THAT THIS FLAMBOYANT YEAR IS THE BEGINNING OF SOCCER'S DECLINE IN THE UNITED STATES.
THE THUNDEROUS SUCCESS OF THIS SPORT LED TO EXTRAVAGANT EXPENDITURES, WHICH INDEBTED THE CLUBS.
AND AGAINST ALL EXPECTATIONS, THE PUBLIC WILL QUICKLY LOSE INTEREST IN SOCCER. A FEW SPECIALISTS ARE ALREADY EXPRESSING A HYPOTHESIS.
WHAT FUTURE IS THERE FOR SOCCER HERE IN THE U.S. WITHOUT THE CHARISMATIC PELÉ?
NONE, I'M VERY AFRAID!
ON OCTOBER 1, 1977, A VERY SYMBOLIC FAREWELL MATCH.
PELE
10
I'M PLAYING THE FIRST HALF WITH THE COSMOS—
THEN THE SECOND WITH THE SANTOS!
PELÉ SCORES HIS FINAL PROFESSIONAL GOAL* WITH HIS FATHER WATCHING FROM THE VIP STANDS.
BOM!
PELÉ IS 37. HE'S CONQUERED THE ENTIRE EARTH, AND FREE FROM WANT, HE CAN FINALLY STOP FOR GOOD.
LOVE! LOVE! LOVE!
THE KING
PELE

*ACCORDING TO THE GUINNESS WORLD RECORDS, HIS TOTAL IS 1,274 GOALS IN PROFESSIONAL MATCHES BETWEEN SEPTEMBER 7, 1956, AND OCTOBER 1, 1977.

Chapter 8
World Ambassador

"Pelé played soccer for twenty-two years, and during that time, he did more for friendship and brotherhood than any other ambassador."
—J. B. Pinheiro, Brazilian ambassador to the United Nations

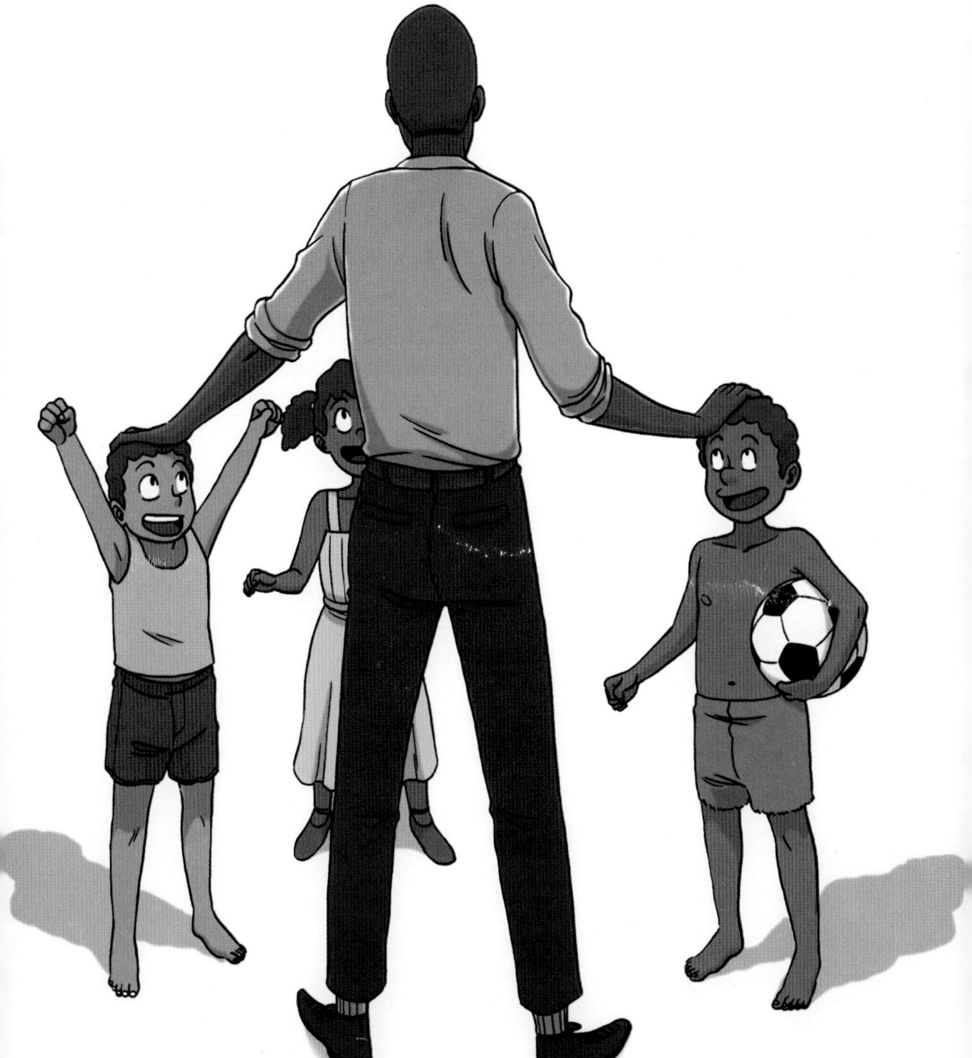

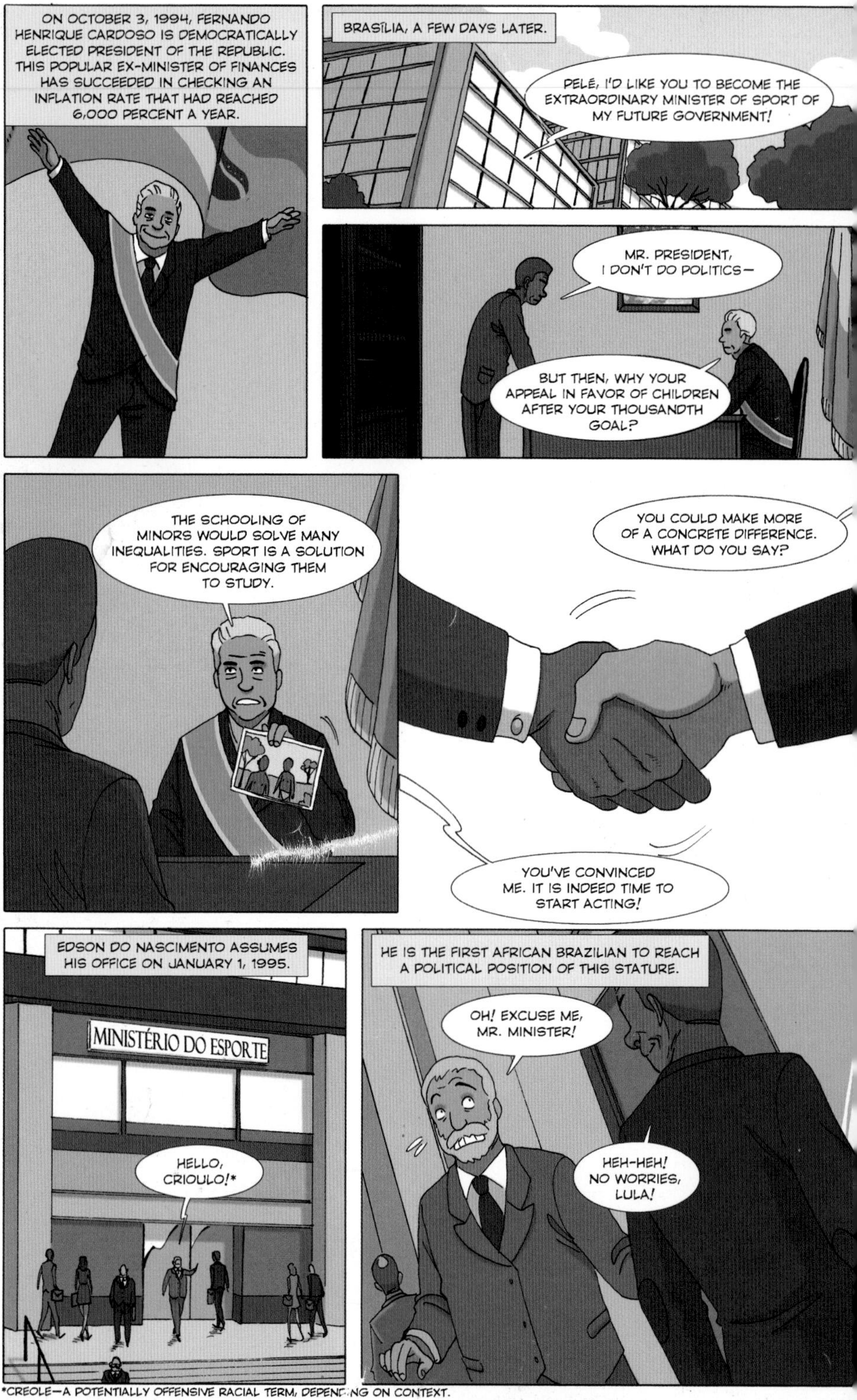
ON OCTOBER 3, 1994, FERNANDO HENRIQUE CARDOSO IS DEMOCRATICALLY ELECTED PRESIDENT OF THE REPUBLIC. THIS POPULAR EX-MINISTER OF FINANCES HAS SUCCEEDED IN CHECKING AN INFLATION RATE THAT HAD REACHED 6,000 PERCENT A YEAR.
BRASÍLIA, A FEW DAYS LATER.
PELÉ, I'D LIKE YOU TO BECOME THE EXTRAORDINARY MINISTER OF SPORT OF MY FUTURE GOVERNMENT!
MR. PRESIDENT, I DON'T DO POLITICS—
BUT THEN, WHY YOUR APPEAL IN FAVOR OF CHILDREN AFTER YOUR THOUSANDTH GOAL?
THE SCHOOLING OF MINORS WOULD SOLVE MANY INEQUALITIES. SPORT IS A SOLUTION FOR ENCOURAGING THEM TO STUDY.
YOU COULD MAKE MORE OF A CONCRETE DIFFERENCE. WHAT DO YOU SAY?
YOU'VE CONVINCED ME. IT IS INDEED TIME TO START ACTING!
EDSON DO NASCIMENTO ASSUMES HIS OFFICE ON JANUARY 1, 1995.
MINISTÉRIO DO ESPORTE
HELLO, CRIOULO!*
HE IS THE FIRST AFRICAN BRAZILIAN TO REACH A POLITICAL POSITION OF THIS STATURE.
OH! EXCUSE ME, MR. MINISTER!
HEH-HEH! NO WORRIES, LULA!

*CREOLE—A POTENTIALLY OFFENSIVE RACIAL TERM, DEPENDING ON CONTEXT.

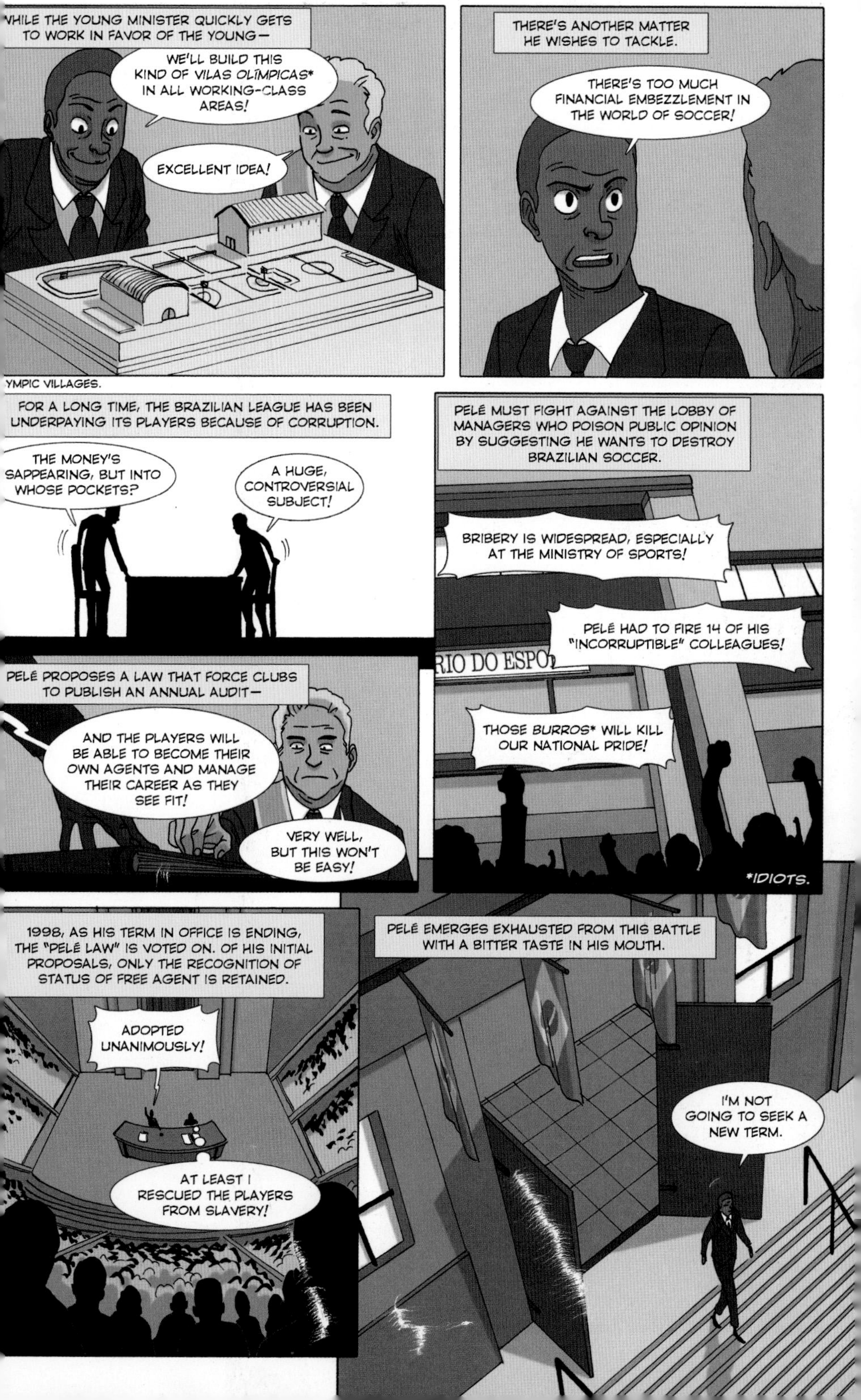

WHILE THE YOUNG MINISTER QUICKLY GETS TO WORK IN FAVOR OF THE YOUNG—
WE'LL BUILD THIS KIND OF VILAS OLÍMPICAS* IN ALL WORKING-CLASS AREAS!
EXCELLENT IDEA!
THERE'S ANOTHER MATTER HE WISHES TO TACKLE.
THERE'S TOO MUCH FINANCIAL EMBEZZLEMENT IN THE WORLD OF SOCCER!
YMPIC VILLAGES.
FOR A LONG TIME, THE BRAZILIAN LEAGUE HAS BEEN UNDERPAYING ITS PLAYERS BECAUSE OF CORRUPTION.
THE MONEY'S SAPPEARING, BUT INTO WHOSE POCKETS?
A HUGE, CONTROVERSIAL SUBJECT!
PELÉ MUST FIGHT AGAINST THE LOBBY OF MANAGERS WHO POISON PUBLIC OPINION BY SUGGESTING HE WANTS TO DESTROY BRAZILIAN SOCCER.
BRIBERY IS WIDESPREAD, ESPECIALLY AT THE MINISTRY OF SPORTS!
PELÉ HAD TO FIRE 14 OF HIS "INCORRUPTIBLE" COLLEAGUES!
RIO DO ESPO
THOSE BURROS* WILL KILL OUR NATIONAL PRIDE!
*IDIOTS.
PELÉ PROPOSES A LAW THAT FORCE CLUBS TO PUBLISH AN ANNUAL AUDIT—
AND THE PLAYERS WILL BE ABLE TO BECOME THEIR OWN AGENTS AND MANAGE THEIR CAREER AS THEY SEE FIT!
VERY WELL, BUT THIS WON'T BE EASY!
1998, AS HIS TERM IN OFFICE IS ENDING, THE "PELÉ LAW" IS VOTED ON. OF HIS INITIAL PROPOSALS, ONLY THE RECOGNITION OF STATUS OF FREE AGENT IS RETAINED.
ADOPTED UNANIMOUSLY!
AT LEAST I RESCUED THE PLAYERS FROM SLAVERY!
PELÉ EMERGES EXHAUSTED FROM THIS BATTLE WITH A BITTER TASTE IN HIS MOUTH.
I'M NOT GOING TO SEEK A NEW TERM.

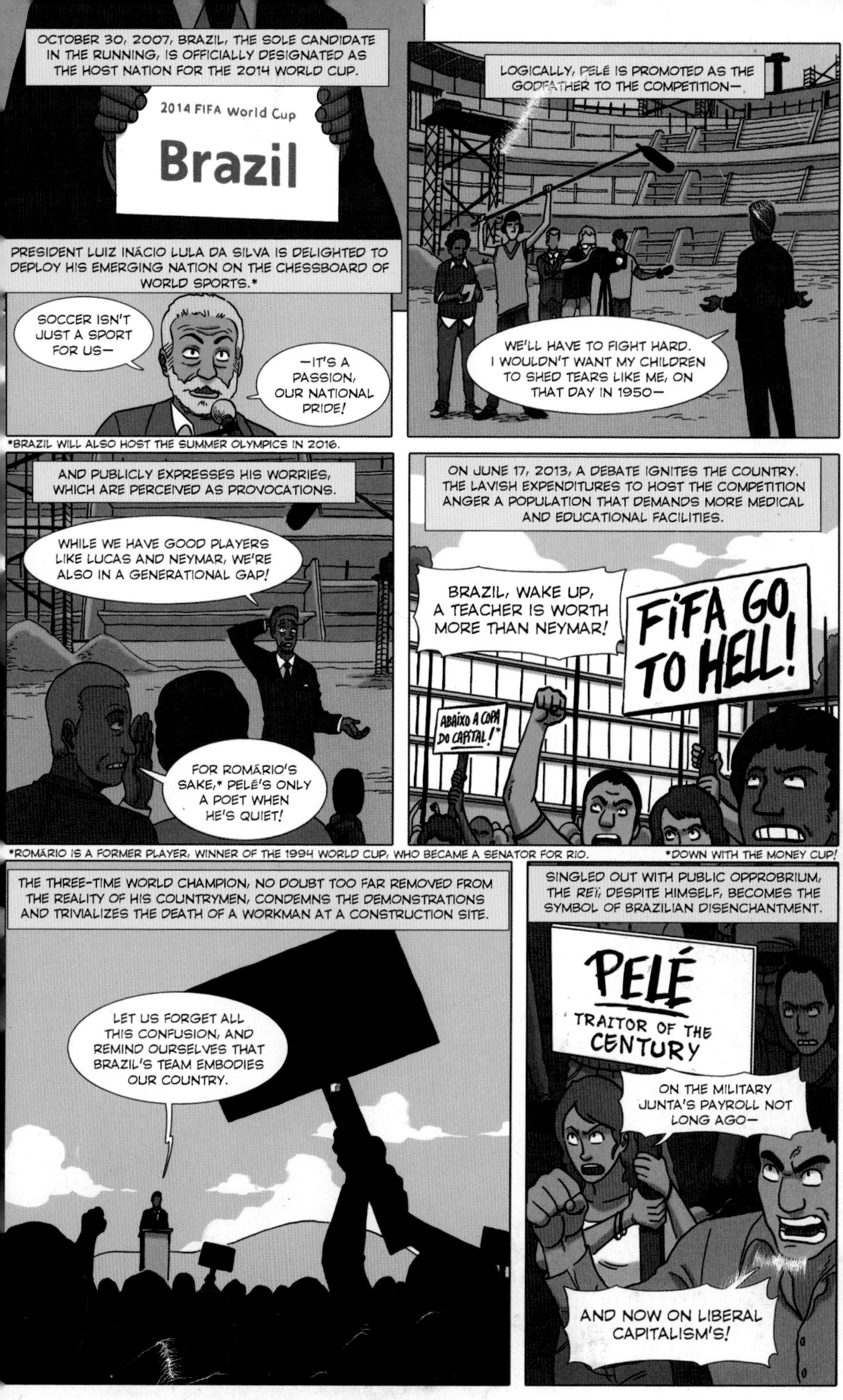

OCTOBER 30, 2007, BRAZIL, THE SOLE CANDIDATE IN THE RUNNING, IS OFFICIALLY DESIGNATED AS THE HOST NATION FOR THE 2014 WORLD CUP.
2014 FIFA World Cup
Brazil
PRESIDENT LUIZ INÁCIO LULA DA SILVA IS DELIGHTED TO DEPLOY HIS EMERGING NATION ON THE CHESSBOARD OF WORLD SPORTS.*
SOCCER ISN'T JUST A SPORT FOR US—
—IT'S A PASSION, OUR NATIONAL PRIDE!
LOGICALLY, PELÉ IS PROMOTED AS THE GODFATHER TO THE COMPETITION—
WE'LL HAVE TO FIGHT HARD. I WOULDN'T WANT MY CHILDREN TO SHED TEARS LIKE ME, ON THAT DAY IN 1950—
*BRAZIL WILL ALSO HOST THE SUMMER OLYMPICS IN 2016.
AND PUBLICLY EXPRESSES HIS WORRIES, WHICH ARE PERCEIVED AS PROVOCATIONS.
WHILE WE HAVE GOOD PLAYERS LIKE LUCAS AND NEYMAR, WE'RE ALSO IN A GENERATIONAL GAP!
FOR ROMÁRIO'S SAKE,* PELÉ'S ONLY A POET WHEN HE'S QUIET!
ON JUNE 17, 2013, A DEBATE IGNITES THE COUNTRY. THE LAVISH EXPENDITURES TO HOST THE COMPETITION ANGER A POPULATION THAT DEMANDS MORE MEDICAL AND EDUCATIONAL FACILITIES.
BRAZIL, WAKE UP, A TEACHER IS WORTH MORE THAN NEYMAR!
FIFA GO TO HELL!
ABAIXO A COPA DO CAPITAL!*
*ROMÁRIO IS A FORMER PLAYER, WINNER OF THE 1994 WORLD CUP, WHO BECAME A SENATOR FOR RIO.
*DOWN WITH THE MONEY CUP!
THE THREE-TIME WORLD CHAMPION, NO DOUBT TOO FAR REMOVED FROM THE REALITY OF HIS COUNTRYMEN, CONDEMNS THE DEMONSTRATIONS AND TRIVIALIZES THE DEATH OF A WORKMAN AT A CONSTRUCTION SITE.
LET US FORGET ALL THIS CONFUSION, AND REMIND OURSELVES THAT BRAZIL'S TEAM EMBODIES OUR COUNTRY.
SINGLED OUT WITH PUBLIC OPPROBRIUM, THE REI, DESPITE HIMSELF, BECOMES THE SYMBOL OF BRAZILIAN DISENCHANTMENT.
PELÉ TRAITOR OF THE CENTURY
ON THE MILITARY JUNTA'S PAYROLL NOT LONG AGO—
AND NOW ON LIBERAL CAPITALISM'S!

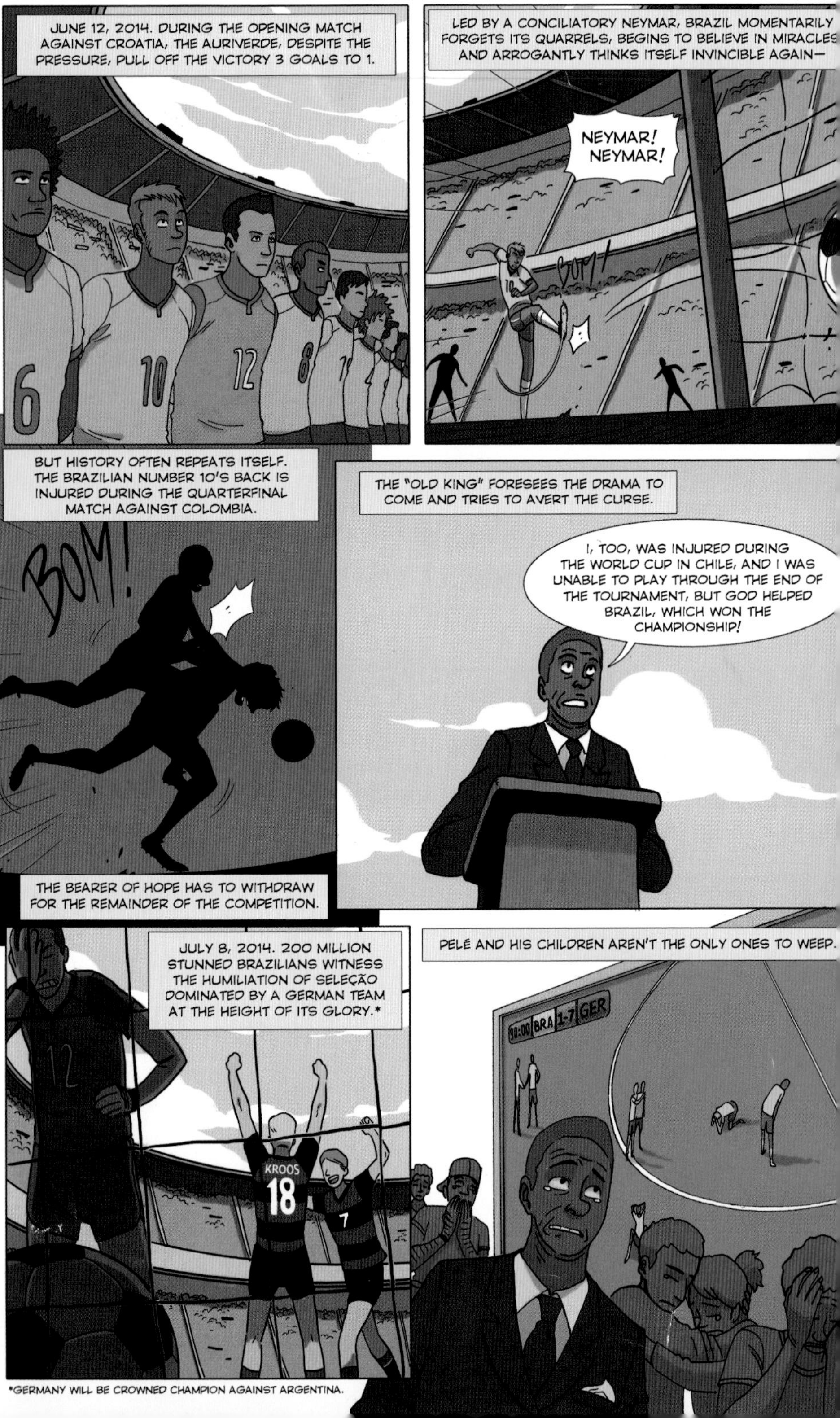
JUNE 12, 2014. DURING THE OPENING MATCH AGAINST CROATIA, THE AURIVERDE, DESPITE THE PRESSURE, PULL OFF THE VICTORY 3 GOALS TO 1.
LED BY A CONCILIATORY NEYMAR, BRAZIL MOMENTARILY FORGETS ITS QUARRELS, BEGINS TO BELIEVE IN MIRACLES AND ARROGANTLY THINKS ITSELF INVINCIBLE AGAIN—
NEYMAR! NEYMAR!
BOM!
BUT HISTORY OFTEN REPEATS ITSELF. THE BRAZILIAN NUMBER 10'S BACK IS INJURED DURING THE QUARTERFINAL MATCH AGAINST COLOMBIA.
BOM!
THE BEARER OF HOPE HAS TO WITHDRAW FOR THE REMAINDER OF THE COMPETITION.
THE "OLD KING" FORESEES THE DRAMA TO COME AND TRIES TO AVERT THE CURSE.
I, TOO, WAS INJURED DURING THE WORLD CUP IN CHILE, AND I WAS UNABLE TO PLAY THROUGH THE END OF THE TOURNAMENT, BUT GOD HELPED BRAZIL, WHICH WON THE CHAMPIONSHIP!
JULY 8, 2014. 200 MILLION STUNNED BRAZILIANS WITNESS THE HUMILIATION OF SELEÇÃO DOMINATED BY A GERMAN TEAM AT THE HEIGHT OF ITS GLORY.*
KROOS
PELÉ AND HIS CHILDREN AREN'T THE ONLY ONES TO WEEP.
BRA 1-7 GER

*GERMANY WILL BE CROWNED CHAMPION AGAINST ARGENTINA.

Extra Time
Sudden-Death Overtime!

"How do you spell Pelé? G-O-D."
—*Sunday Times,* 1970

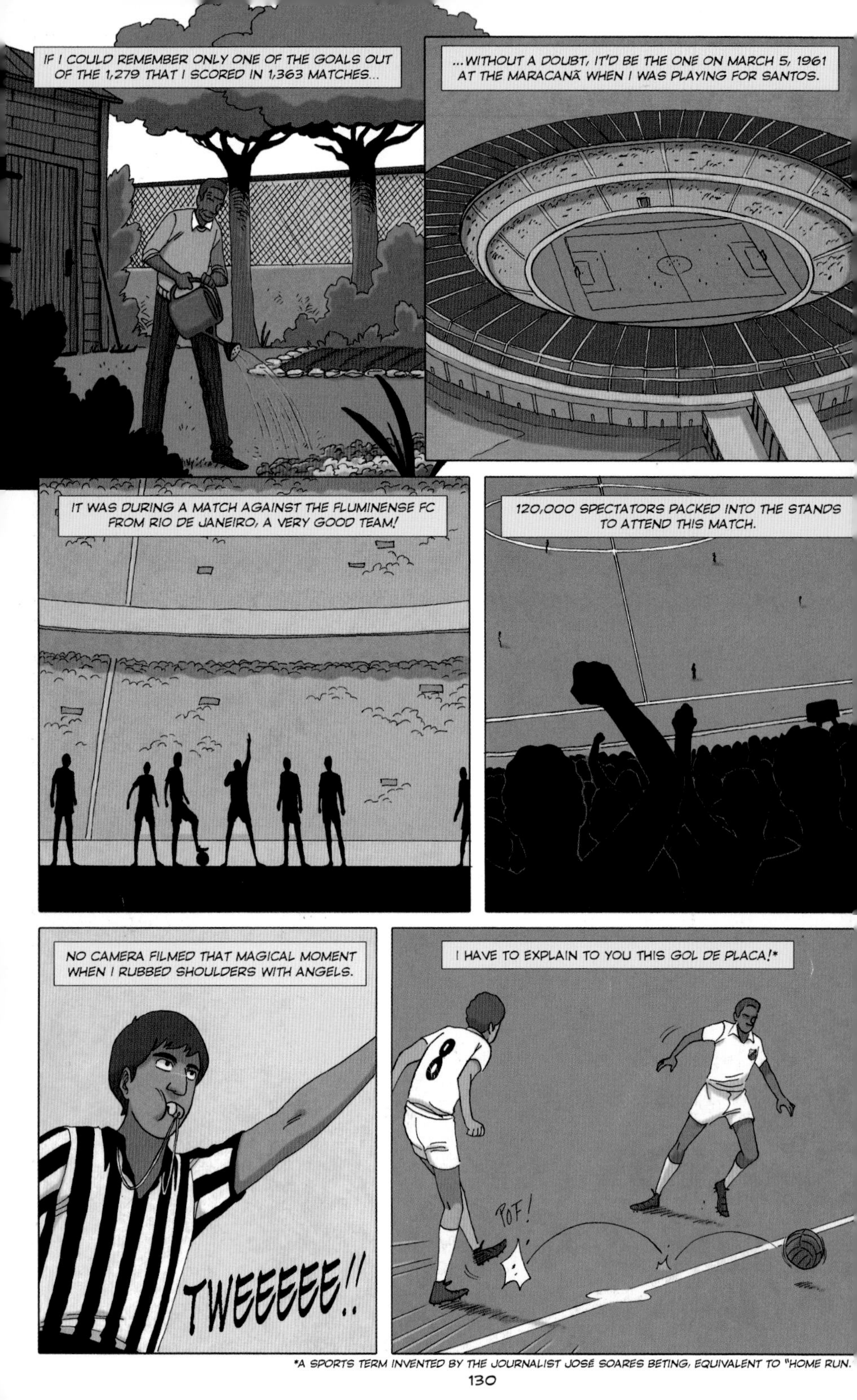
IF I COULD REMEMBER ONLY ONE OF THE GOALS OUT OF THE 1,279 THAT I SCORED IN 1,363 MATCHES...
...WITHOUT A DOUBT, IT'D BE THE ONE ON MARCH 5, 1961 AT THE MARACANÃ WHEN I WAS PLAYING FOR SANTOS.
IT WAS DURING A MATCH AGAINST THE FLUMINENSE FC FROM RIO DE JANEIRO, A VERY GOOD TEAM!
120,000 SPECTATORS PACKED INTO THE STANDS TO ATTEND THIS MATCH.
NO CAMERA FILMED THAT MAGICAL MOMENT WHEN I RUBBED SHOULDERS WITH ANGELS.
TWEEEEE!!
I HAVE TO EXPLAIN TO YOU THIS GOL DE PLACA!*
POF!

*A SPORTS TERM INVENTED BY THE JOURNALIST JOSÉ SOARES BETING, EQUIVALENT TO "HOME RUN.

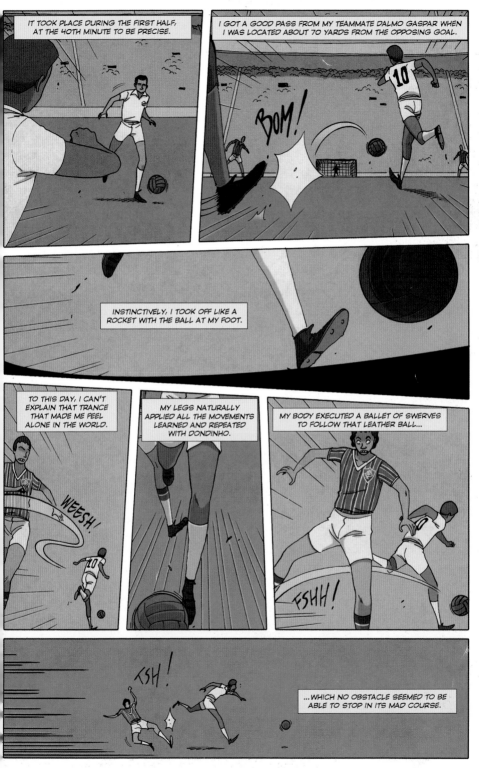

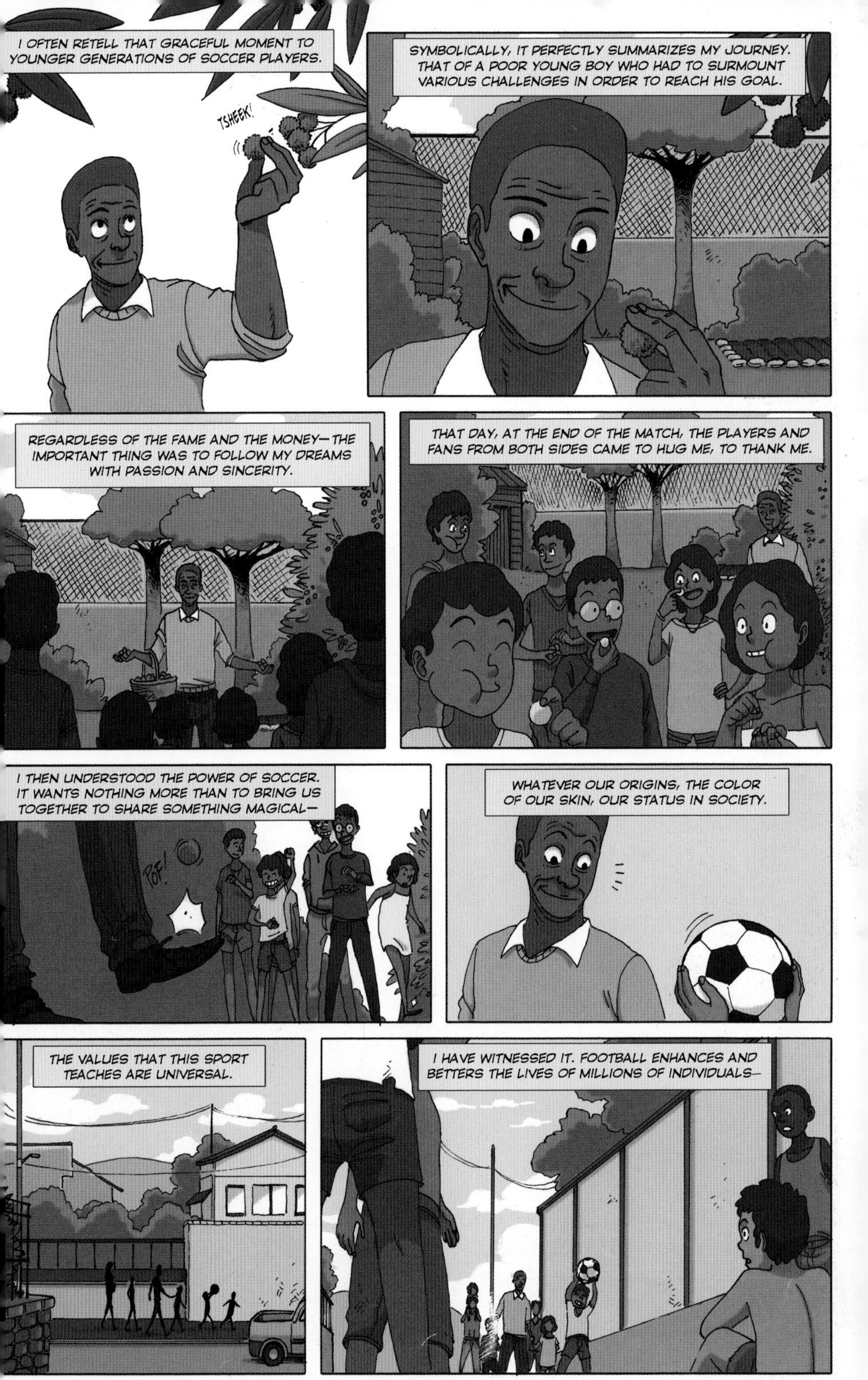
I OFTEN RETELL THAT GRACEFUL MOMENT TO YOUNGER GENERATIONS OF SOCCER PLAYERS.
TSHEEK!
SYMBOLICALLY, IT PERFECTLY SUMMARIZES MY JOURNEY. THAT OF A POOR YOUNG BOY WHO HAD TO SURMOUNT VARIOUS CHALLENGES IN ORDER TO REACH HIS GOAL.
REGARDLESS OF THE FAME AND THE MONEY—THE IMPORTANT THING WAS TO FOLLOW MY DREAMS WITH PASSION AND SINCERITY.
THAT DAY, AT THE END OF THE MATCH, THE PLAYERS AND FANS FROM BOTH SIDES CAME TO HUG ME, TO THANK ME.
I THEN UNDERSTOOD THE POWER OF SOCCER. IT WANTS NOTHING MORE THAN TO BRING US TOGETHER TO SHARE SOMETHING MAGICAL—
POF!
WHATEVER OUR ORIGINS, THE COLOR OF OUR SKIN, OUR STATUS IN SOCIETY.
THE VALUES THAT THIS SPORT TEACHES ARE UNIVERSAL.
I HAVE WITNESSED IT. FOOTBALL ENHANCES AND BETTERS THE LIVES OF MILLIONS OF INDIVIDUALS—

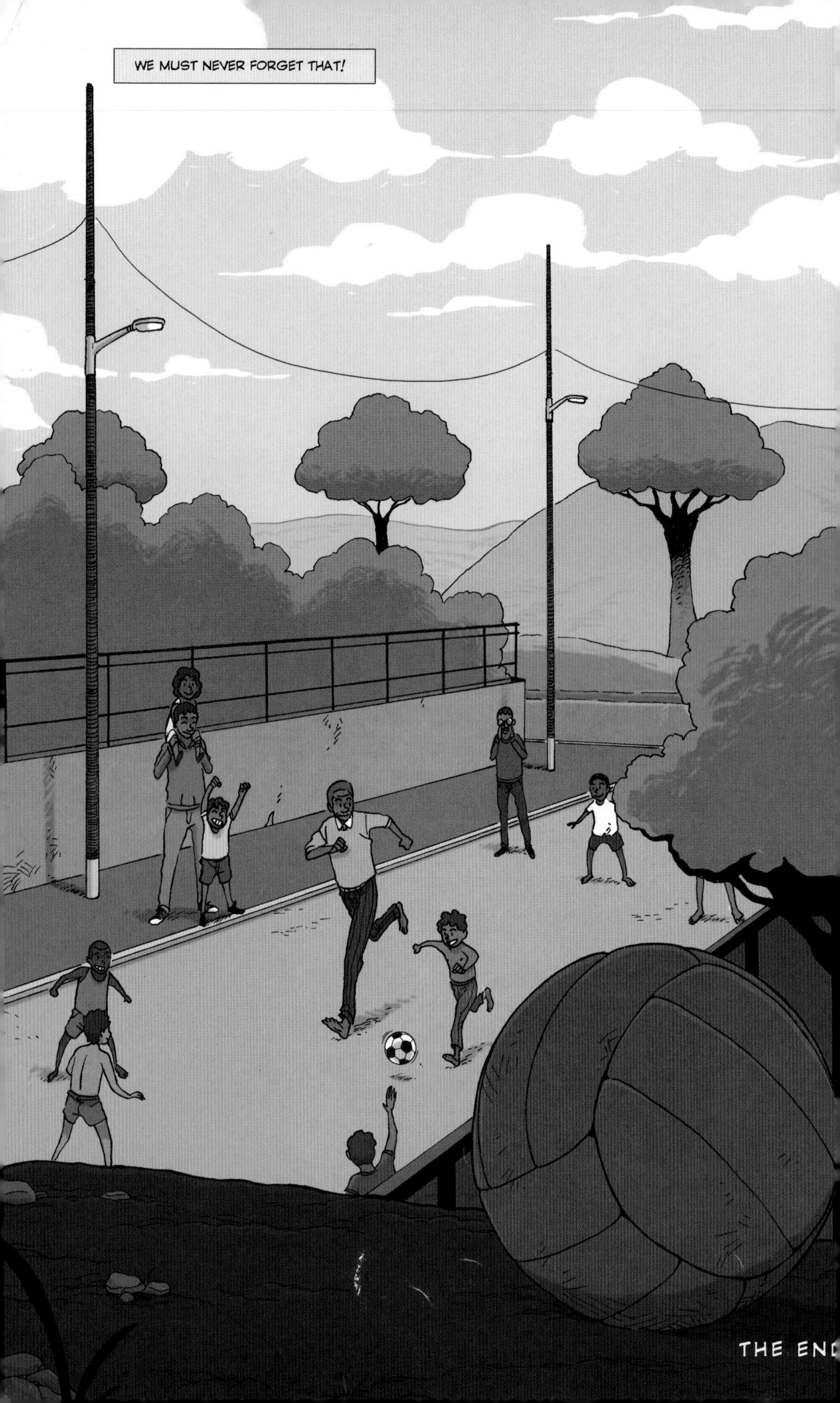
WE MUST NEVER FORGET THAT!
THE END

Pelé, NASL Soccer—1975
By Jerry Cooke / Sports Illustrated
© Getty Images

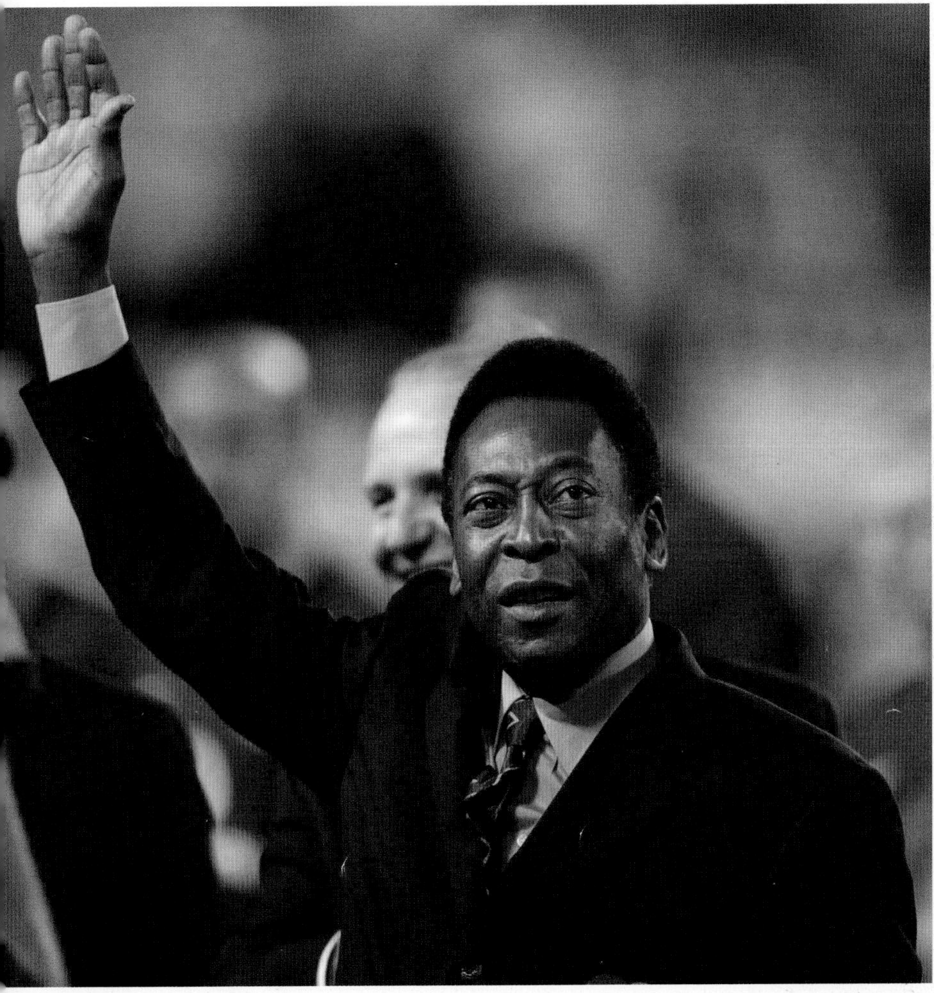

ělé—2003
Rex / Shutterstock

"I'm not afraid of dying, because I have three hearts.
I was born in 'Três Corações' [Three Hearts], don't forget!
After my death, I'd like people to remember I was a good person
who always wanted to bring people of all kinds together.
And that they also remember that I was—a good player!"

Edson Arantes do Nascimento, or "Pelé"

First Second

English translation by Joe Johnson
English translation © 2017 by Roaring Brook Press,
a division of Holtzbrink Publishing Holdings Limited Partnership

Published by First Second
First Second is an imprint of Roaring Brook Press, a division
of Holtzbrinck Publishing Holdings Limited Partnership
175 Fifth Avenue, New York, New York 10010
All rights reserved

Library of Congress Control Number: 2016961595

Paperback ISBN: 978-1-62672-755-7
Hardcover ISBN: 978-1-62672-979-7

Our books may be purchased in bulk for promotional, educational, or business use. Please
contact your local bookseller or the Macmillan Corporate and Premium Sales Department
at (800) 221-7945 ext. 5442 or by e-mail at MacmillanSpecialMarkets@macmillan.com.

FIRST
EDITION

Originally published in 2016 in French by 21g, a division of Blue Lotus Prod
as *Le Roi Pelé - L'Homme et la Légende* © 2016 by Blue Lotus Prod

First American edition 2017
Book design by Gordon Whiteside

Printed in China by RR Donnelly Asia Printing Solutions Ltd.,
Dongguan City, Guangdong Province
Paperback: 10 9 8 7 6 5 4 3 2 1
Hardcover: 10 9 8 7 6 5 4 3 2 1

BY ART
WE LIVE